Overcoming
Grief
and Trauma

Overcoming Grief and Trauma

Strategic Pastoral Counseling Resources

Mel Lawrenz and Daniel Green

Baker Books

A Division of Baker Book House Co
Grand Rapids, Michigan 49516

Published by Baker Books
a division of Baker Book House Company
PO Box 6287, Grand Rapids, Michigan 49516-6287

Printed in the United States of America

Library of Congress Cataloging-in-Publication Data

Lawrenz, Mel.
    Overcoming grief and trauma / Mel Lawrenz and Daniel Green.
      p. cm. — (Strategic pastoral counseling resources)
    Includes bibliographical references.
    ISBN 0-8010-1056-X
    1. Grief—Religious aspects—Christianity. 2. Psychic trauma. 3. Pastoral counseling. I. Green, Daniel (Daniel R.) II. Title. III. Series.
BV4905.2.L285   1995
259'.6—dc20   95-33295

to the mourners
who would be comforters
—2 Corinthians 1:3ff.

Contents

Acknowledgments

There are many people—teachers, coworkers, authors of books—who may be acknowledged as having taught us about grief and trauma.

But it is the participants themselves, the mourners, who deserve more credit than anyone. As a pastor and a psychologist we have many opportunities to meet people who suddenly come to a time of serious loss in life, and then have begun the journey of grieving. A great many of them express along the way the desire to be able to help other people going through loss in their lives. They have and they are. Their experience is part and parcel of this work. In particular, our friend Mary Haynes, in the three years in which she battled the cancer that eventually defeated her body at age 29, gave the reality of pain and loss, and also of God's grace and truth.

Our wives, Ingrid and Lynne, helped not only in their support but in their active, thoughtful involvement in the development of the central ideas of this book.

Final thanks to the editorial staff of Baker Books and to the staffs of Elmbrook Church and New Life Resources, Inc., with whom we have the privilege of working.

An Introduction to Strategic Pastoral Counseling

David G. Benner

While the provision of spiritual counsel has been an integral part of Christian soul care since the earliest days of the church, the contemporary understanding and practice of pastoral counseling is largely a product of the twentieth century. Developing within the shadow of the modern psychotherapies, pastoral counseling has derived much of its style and approach from these clinical therapeutics. What this has meant is that pastoral counselors have often seen themselves more as counselors than as pastors and the counseling that they have provided has often been a rather awkward adaptation of clinical counseling models to a pastoral context. This, in turn, has often resulted in significant tension between the pastoral and psychological dimensions of the counseling provided by clergy and others in Christian ministry. It is also frequently reflected in pastoral counselors who are more interested in anything connected with the modern mystery cult of psychotherapy than with their own tradition of Christian soul care, and who, as a consequence, are often quite insecure in their pastoral role and identity.

While pastoral counseling owes much to the psychological culture that has gained ascendancy in the West during the past century, this influence has quite clearly been a mixed blessing. Contemporary pastoral counselors typically offer their help with much more psychological sophistication than was the case several decades ago, but all too often they do so without a clear sense of the uniqueness of counseling that is offered by a pastor. And not only are the distinctive spiritual resources of Christian ministry often deemphasized or ignored, but the tensions that are associated with attempts to directly translate clinical models of counseling into the pastoral context become a source of much frustration. This is in part why so many pastors report dissatisfaction with their counseling. While they indicate that this dissatisfaction is a result of insufficient training in and time for counseling, a bigger part of the problem may be that pastors have been offered approaches to counseling that are of questionable appropriateness for the pastoral context and that will inevitably leave them feeling frustrated and inadequate.

Strategic Pastoral Counseling is a model of counseling that has been specifically designed to fit the role, resources, and needs of the typical pastor who counsels. Information about this "typical" pastor was solicited by means of a survey of over 400 pastors (this research is described in the introductory volume of the series, *Strategic Pastoral Counseling: A Short-Term Structured Model* [Benner, 1992]). The model appropriates the insights of contemporary counseling theory without sacrificing the resources of pastoral ministry. Furthermore, it takes its form and direction from the pastoral role and in so doing offers an approach to counseling that is not only congruent with the other aspects of pastoral ministry but that places pastoral counseling at the very heart of ministry.

The present volume represents an application of Strategic Pastoral Counseling to one commonly encountered problem situation. As such, it presupposes a familiarity with the basic model. Readers not familiar with *Strategic Pastoral Counseling: A Short-Term Structured Model* should consult this book for a detailed presentation of the model and its implementation. What follows is a brief review of this material which, while it does not adequately summarize all that is presented in that book, should serve as a reminder of the most important features of the Strategic Pastoral Counseling approach.

The Strategic Pastoral Counseling Model

Strategic Pastoral Counseling is short-term, bibliotherapeutic, wholistic, structured, spiritually focused, and explicitly Christian. Each of these characteristics will be briefly discussed in order.

Short-Term Counseling

Counseling can be brief (that is, conducted over a relatively few sessions), time-limited (that is, conducted within an initially fixed number of total sessions), or both. Strategic Pastoral Counseling is both brief and time-limited, working within a suggested maximum of five sessions. The decision to set this upper limit on the number of sessions was in response to the fact that the background research conducted in the design of the model indicated that 87 percent of the pastoral counseling conducted by pastors in general ministry involves five sessions or less. This short-term approach to counseling seems ideally suited to the time availability, training, and role demands of pastors.

Recent research in short-term counseling has made it clear that while such an approach requires that the counselor be diligent in maintaining the focus on the single agreed upon central problem, significant and enduring changes can occur through a very small number of counseling sessions. Strategic Pastoral Counseling differs, in this regard, from the more ongoing relationship of discipleship or spiritual guidance. In these, the goal is the development of spiritual maturity. Strategic Pastoral Counseling has a much more modest goal: examining a particular problem or experience in the light of God's will for and activity in the life of the individual seeking help and attempting to facilitate growth in and through that person's present life situation. While this is still an ambitious goal, its focused nature makes it quite attainable within a short period of time. It is this focus that makes the counseling strategic.

The five-session limit should be communicated by the pastor no later than the first session and preferably in the prior conversation when the time is set for this session. This ensures that the parishioner is aware of the time limit from the beginning and can share responsibility in keeping the counseling sessions focused. Some people will undoubtedly require more than five sessions in order to bring about a resolution of their problems. These people should be referred to someone who is appropriately qualified for such work; preparation for this referral will be one of the goals of the five sessions. However, the fact that such people may require more help than can be provided in five sessions of pastoral counseling does not mean that they cannot benefit from such focused short-term pastoral care; no individuals should be regarded as inappropriate candidates for Strategic Pastoral Counseling merely because they may require other help.

One final but important note about the suggested limit of five sessions is that this does not have to be tied to a corresponding period of five weeks. In fact, many pastors find weekly sessions to be less useful than sessions scheduled two or three weeks apart. This sort of spacing of the last couple of sessions is particularly helpful and should be considered even if the first several sessions are held weekly.

Bibliotherapeutic Counseling

Bibliotherapy refers to the therapeutic use of reading. Strategic Pastoral Counseling builds the use of written materials into the heart of its approach to pastoral caregiving. The Bible itself is, of course, a rich bibliotherapeutic resource and the encouragement of and direction in its reading is an important part of Strategic Pastoral Counseling. Its use must be disciplined and selective and particular care must be taken to ensure that it is never employed in a mechanical or impersonal manner. However, when used appropriately it can unquestionably be one of the most dynamic and powerful resources available to the pastor who counsels.

While the Bible is a unique bibliotherapeutic resource, it is not the only such resource. Strategic Pastoral Counseling comes with a built-in set of specifically designed resources. Each of the ten volumes in this series has an accompanying book written for the parishioner who is being seen in counseling. These resource books are written by the same authors as the volumes for pastors and are designed for easy integration into counseling sessions.

The use of reading materials that are consistent with the counseling being provided can serve as a most significant support and extension of the counseling offered by a pastor. The parishioner now has a helping resource that is not limited by the pastor's time and availability. Furthermore, the pastor can now allow the written materials to do part of the work of counseling, using the sessions to deal with those matters that are not as well addressed through the written page.

Wholistic Counseling

It might seem surprising to suggest that a short-term counseling approach should also be wholistic. But this is both possible and highly desirable. Wholistic counseling is counseling that is responsive to the totality of the complex psycho-spiritual dynamics that make up the life of human persons. Biblical psychology is clearly a wholistic psychology. The various "parts" of persons (i.e., body, soul, spirit, heart, flesh, etc.) are never presented as separate faculties or independent components of persons but always as different ways of seeing the whole person. Biblical discussions of persons emphasize first and foremost their essential unity of being. Humans are ultimately understandable only in the light of this primary and irreducible wholeness and helping efforts that are truly Christian must resist the temptation to see persons only through their thoughts, feelings, behaviors, or any other single manifestation of being.

The alternative to wholism in counseling is to focus on only one of these modalities of functioning and this is, indeed, what many approaches to counseling do. In contrast, Strategic Pastoral Counseling asserts that pastoral counseling must be responsive to the behavioral (action), cognitive (thought), and affective (feeling) elements of personal functioning. Each examined separately can obscure that which is really going on with a person. But taken together they form the basis for a comprehensive assessment and effective intervention. Strategic Pastoral Counseling provides a framework for ensuring that each of these spheres of functioning is addressed and this, in fact, provides much of the structure for the counseling.

Structured Counseling

The structured nature of Strategic Pastoral Counseling is that which enables its brevity, ensuring that each of the sessions has a clear focus and that each builds upon the previous ones in contributing toward the accomplishment of the overall goals. The framework that structures Strategic Pastoral Counseling is sufficiently tight as to enable the pastor to provide a wholistic assessment and counseling intervention within a maximum of five sessions and yet it is also sufficiently flexible to allow for differences in individual styles of different counselors. This is very important because Strategic Pastoral Counseling is not primarily a set of techniques but an intimate encounter of and dialogue between people.

The structure of Strategic Pastoral Counseling grows out of the goal of addressing the feelings, thoughts, and behaviors that are part of the troubling experiences of the person seeking help. It is also a structure that is responsive to the several tasks that face the pastoral counselor, tasks such as conducting an initial assessment, developing a general understanding of the problem and of the person's major needs, and selecting and delivering interventions and resources that will bring help. This structure is described in more detail later.

Spiritually Focused Counseling

The fourth distinctive of Strategic Pastoral Counseling is that it is spiritually focused. This does not mean that only religious matters are discussed. Our spirituality is our essential heart commitments, our basic life direction, and our fundamental allegiances. These spiritual aspects of our being are, of course, reflected in our attitudes toward God and are expressed in our explicitly religious values and behaviors. However, they are also reflected in matters that may seem on the surface to be much less religious. Strategic Pastoral Counselors place a primacy on listening to this underlying spiritual story. They listen for what we might call the story behind the story.

But listening to the story behind the story requires that one first listen to and take seriously the presenting story. To disregard the presenting situation is spiritualization of a problem. It fails to take the problem seriously and makes a mockery of counseling as genuine dialogue. The Strategic Pastoral Counselor thus listens to and enters into the experience of parishioners as they relate their struggles and life's experiences. But while this is a real part of the story, it is not the whole story that must be heard and understood. For in the midst of this story emerges another: the story of their spiritual response to these experiences. This response may be one of unwavering trust in God but a failure to expect much of him. Or it may be one of doubt, anger, confusion, or despair. Each of these is a spiritual response to present struggles and in one form or another, the spiritual aspect of the person's experience will always be discernible to the pastor who watches for it. Strategic Pastoral Counseling makes this underlying spiritual story the primary focus.

Explicitly Christian Counseling

While it is important to not confuse spirituality with religiosity, it is equally important to not confuse Christian spirituality with any of its imitations. In this regard, it is crucial that Strategic Pastoral Counseling be distinctively and explicitly Christian. And while Strategic Pastoral Counseling begins with a focus on spiritual matters understood broadly, its master goal is to facilitate the other person's awareness of and response to the call of God to surrender and service. This is the essential and most important distinctive of Strategic Pastoral Counseling.

One of the ways in which Strategic Pastoral Counseling is made explicitly Christian is through its utilization of Christian theological language, images, and concepts and the religious resources of prayer, Scripture, and the sacraments. These resources must never be used in a mechanical, legalistic, or magical fashion. But used sensitively and wisely, they can be the conduit for a dynamic contact between God and the person seeking pastoral help. And this is the goal of their utilization, not some superficial baptizing of the counseling in order to make it Christian but rather a way of bringing the one seeking help more closely in touch with the God who is the source of all life, growth, and healing.

Another important resource that is appropriated by the Strategic Pastoral Counselor is that of the church as a community. Too often pastoral counseling is conducted in a way that is not appreciably different from that which might be offered by a Christian counselor in private practice. This most unfortunate practice ignores the rich resources that are potentially available in any Christian congregation. One of the most important ways in which Strategic Pastoral Counseling is able to maintain its short-term nature is by the pastor connecting the person seeking help with others in the church who can provide portions of that help. The congregation can, of course, also be involved in less individualistic ways. Support and ministry groups of various sorts are becoming a part of many congregations that seek to provide a dynamic ministry to their community and are potentially important resources for the Strategic Pastoral Counselor.

A final and even more fundamental way in which Strategic Pastoral Counseling is Christian is in the reliance on the Holy Spirit that it encourages. The Spirit is the indispensable source of all wisdom that is necessary for the practice of pastoral counseling. Recognizing that all healing and growth are ultimately of God, the Strategic Pastoral Counselor can thus take comfort in this reliance on the Spirit of God and on the fact that ultimate responsibility for people and their well-being lies with God.

Stages and Tasks of Strategic Pastoral Counseling

The three overall stages that organize Strategic Pastoral Counseling can be described as *encounter, engagement,* and *disengagement.* The first stage of Strategic Pastoral Counseling, encounter, corresponds to the initial session in which the goal is to establish personal contact with the person seeking help, set the boundaries for the counseling relationship, become acquainted with that person and the central concerns, conduct a pastoral diagnosis, and develop a mutually acceptable focus for the subsequent sessions. The second stage, engagement, involves the pastor moving beyond the first contact and establishing a deeper working alliance with the person seeking help. This normally occupies the next one to three sessions and entails the exploration of the person's feelings, thoughts, and behavioral patterns associated with this problem area and the development of new perspectives and strategies for coping or change. The third and final stage, disengagement, describes the focus of the last one or possibly two sessions, and involves an evaluation of progress and an assessment of remaining concerns, the making of a referral for further help if this is needed, and the ending of the counseling relationship. These stages and tasks are summarized in the table below.

Stages and Tasks of Strategic Pastoral Counseling

Stage 1:   Encounter (Session 1)
* Joining and boundary-setting
* Exploring the central concerns and relevant history
* Conducting a pastoral diagnosis
* Achieving a mutually agreeable focus for counseling

Stage 2:   Engagement (Sessions 2, 3, 4)
* Exploration of cognitive, affective, and behavioral aspects of the problem and the identification of resources for coping or change

Stage 3:   Disengagement (Session 5)
* Evaluation of progress and assessment of remaining concerns
* Referral (if needed)
* Termination of counseling

The Encounter Stage

The first task in this initial stage of Strategic Pastoral Counseling is joining and boundary-setting. Joining involves putting the parishioner at ease by means of a few moments of casual conversation that is designed to ease pastor and parishioner into contact. Such preliminary conversation should never take more than five minutes and should usually be kept to two or three. It will not always be necessary, because some people are immediately ready to tell their story. Boundary-setting involves the communication of the purpose of this session and the time frame for the session and your work together. This should not normally require more than a sentence or two.

The exploration of central concerns and relevant history usually begins with an invitation for parishioners to describe what led them to seek help at the present time. After hearing an expression of these immediate concerns, it is usually helpful to get a brief historical perspective on these concerns and the person. Ten to fifteen minutes of exploration of the course of development of the presenting problems and their efforts to cope or get help with them is the foundation of this part of the session. It is also important at this point to get some idea of the parishioner's present living and family arrangements as well as work and/or educational situation. The organizing thread for this section of the first interview should be the presenting problem. These matters will not be the only ones discussed but this focus serves to give the session the necessary direction.

Stripped of its distracting medical connotations, diagnosis is problem definition and this is a fundamental part of any approach to counseling. Diagnoses involve judgments about the nature of the problem and, either implicitly or explicitly, pastoral counselors make such judgments every time they commence a counseling relationship. But in order for diagnoses to be relevant they must guide the counseling that will follow. This means that the categories of pastoral assessment must be primarily related to the spiritual focus, which is foundational to any counseling that is appropriately called pastoral. Thus, the diagnosis called for in the first stage of Strategic Pastoral Counseling involves an assessment of the person's spiritual well-being.

The framework for pastoral diagnosis adopted by Strategic Pastoral Counseling is that suggested by Malony (1988) and used as the basis of his Religious Status Interview. Malony proposed that the diagnosis of Christian religious well-being should involve the assessment of the person's awareness of God, acceptance of God's grace, repentance and responsibility, response to God's leadership and direction, involvement in the church, experience of fellowship, ethics, and openness in the faith. While this approach to pastoral diagnosis has been found to be helpful by many, the Strategic Pastoral Counselor need not feel confined by it. It is offered as a suggested framework for conducting a pastoral assessment and each individual pastoral counselor needs to approach this task in ways that fit his or her own theological convictions and personal style. Further details on conducting a pastoral assessment can be found in *Strategic Pastoral Counseling: A Short-Term Structured Model.*

The final task of the encounter stage of Strategic Pastoral Counseling is achieving a mutually agreeable focus for counseling. Often this is self-evident, made immediately clear by the first expression of the parishioner. At other times parishioners will report a wide range of concerns in the first session and will have to be asked what should constitute the primary problem focus. The identification of the primary problem focus leads naturally to a formulation of goals for the counseling. These goals will sometimes be quite specific (i.e., to be able to make an informed decision about a potential job change) but will also at times be rather broad (i.e., to be able to express feelings related to an illness). As is illustrated in these examples, some goals will describe an end-point while others will describe more of a process. Maintaining this flexibility in how goals are understood is crucial if Strategic Pastoral Counseling is to be a helpful counseling approach for the broad range of situations faced by the pastoral counselor.

The Engagement Stage

The second stage of Strategic Pastoral Counseling involves the further engagement of the pastor and the one seeking help around the problems and concerns that brought them together. This is the heart of the counseling process. The major tasks of this stage are the exploration of the person's feelings, thoughts, and behavioral patterns associated with the central concerns and the development of new perspectives and strategies for coping or change.

It is important to note that the work of this stage may well begin in the first session. The model should not be interpreted in a rigid or mechanical manner. If the goals of the first stage are completed with time remaining in the first session, one can very appropriately begin to move into the tasks of this next stage. However, once the tasks of Stage 1 are completed, those associated with this second stage become the central focus. If the full five sessions of Strategic Pastoral Counseling are employed, this second stage normally provides the structure for sessions 2, 3, and 4.

The central foci for the three sessions normally associated with this stage are the feelings, thoughts, and behaviors associated with the problem presented by the person seeking help. Although these are usually intertwined, a selective focus on each, one at a time, ensures that each is adequately addressed and that all the crucial dynamics of the person's psychospiritual functioning are considered.

The reason for beginning with feelings is that this is where most people themselves begin when they come to a counselor. But this does not mean that most people know their feelings. The exploration of feelings involves encouraging people to face and express whatever it is that they are feeling, to the end that these feelings can be known and then dealt with appropriately. The goal at this point is to listen and respond empathically to the feelings of those seeking help, not to try to change them.

After an exploration of the major feelings being experienced by the person seeking help, the next task is an exploration of the thoughts associated with these feelings and the development of alternative ways of understanding present experiences. It is in this phase of Strategic Pastoral Counseling that the explicit use of Scripture is usually most appropriate. Bearing in mind the potential misuses and problems that can be associated with such use of religious resources, the pastoral counselor should be, nonetheless, open to a direct presentation of scriptural truths when they offer the possibility of a new and helpful perspective on one's situation.

The final task of the engagement stage of Strategic Pastoral Counseling grows directly out of this work on understanding and involves the exploration of the behavioral components of the person's functioning. Here the pastor explores what concrete things the person is doing in the face of the problems or distressing situations being encountered and together with the parishioner begins to identify changes in behavior that may be desirable. The goal of this stage is to identify changes that both pastor and parishioner agree are important and to begin to establish concrete strategies for making these changes.

The Disengagement Stage

The last session or two involves preparation for the termination of counseling and includes two specific tasks: the evaluation of progress and assessment of remaining concerns, and making arrangements regarding a referral if this is needed.

The evaluation of progress is usually a process that both pastor and parishioner will find rewarding. Some of this may be done during previous sessions. Even when this is the case, it is a good idea to use the last session to undertake a brief review of what has been learned from the counseling. Closely associated with this, of course, is an identification of remaining concerns. Seldom is everything resolved after five sessions. This means that the parishioner is preparing to leave counseling with some work yet to be done. But he or she does so with plans for the future and the development of these is an important task of the disengagement stage of Strategic Pastoral Counseling.

If significant problems remain at this point, the last couple of sessions should also be used to make referral arrangements. Ideally these should be discussed in the second or third session and they should by now be all arranged. It might even be ideal if by this point the parishioner could have had a first session with the new counselor, thus allowing a processing of this first experience as part of the final pastoral counseling session.

Recognition of one's own limitations of time, experience, training, and ability is an indispensable component of the practice of all professionals. Pastors are no exception. Pastors offering Strategic Pastoral Counseling need, therefore, to be aware of the resources within their community and be prepared to refer parishioners for help that they can better receive elsewhere.

In the vast majority of cases, the actual termination of a Strategic Pastoral Counseling relationship goes very smoothly. Most often both pastor and parishioner agree that there is no further need to meet and they find easy agreement with, even if some sadness around, the decision to discontinue the counseling sessions. However, there may be times when this process is somewhat difficult. This will sometimes be due to the parishioner's desire to continue to meet. At other times the difficulty in terminating will reside within the pastor. Regardless, the best course of action is usually to follow through on the initial limits agreed upon by both parties.

The exception to this rule is a situation where the parishioner is facing some significant stress or crisis at the end of the five sessions and where there are no other available resources to provide the support needed. If this is the situation, an extension of a few sessions may be appropriate. However, this should again be time-limited and should take the form of crisis management. It should not involve more sessions than is absolutely necessary to restore some degree of stability or to introduce the parishioner to other people who can be of assistance.

Conclusion

Strategic Pastoral Counseling provides a framework for pastors who seek to counsel in a way that is congruent with the rest of their pastoral responsibilities, psychologically informed and responsible. While skill in implementing the model comes only over time, because the approach is focused and time-limited it is quite possible for most pastors to acquire these skills. However, counseling skills cannot be adequately learned simply by reading books. As with all interpersonal skills, they must be learned through practice, and ideally, this practice is best acquired in a context of supervisory feedback from a more experienced pastoral counselor.

The pastor who has mastered the skills of Strategic Pastoral Counseling is in a position to proclaim the Word of God in a highly personalized and relevant manner to people who are often desperate for help. This is a unique and richly rewarding opportunity. Rather than scattering seed in a broadcast manner across ground that is often stony and hard even if at places it is also fertile and receptive to growth, the pastoral counselor has the opportunity to carefully plant one seed at a time. Knowing the soil conditions, he or she is also able to plant it in a highly individualized manner, taking pains to ensure that it will not be quickly blown away, and then gently watering and nourishing its growth. This is the unique opportunity for the ministry of Strategic Pastoral Counseling. It is my prayer that pastors will see the centrality of counseling to their call to ministry, feel encouraged by the presence of an approach to pastoral counseling that lies within their skills and time availability, and will take up these responsibilities with renewed vigor and clarity of direction.

1

Defining Grief and Trauma

To love at all is to be vulnerable. Love anything, and your heart will certainly be wrung and possibly be broken. If you want to make sure of keeping it intact, you must give your heart to no one ... It will not be broken; it will become unbreakable, impenetrable, irredeemable. The alternative to tragedy, or at least to the risk of tragedy, is damnation. The only place outside Heaven where you can be perfectly safe from all the dangers and perturbations of love is Hell.

—C. S. Lewis, *The Four Loves*

The Face of Grief and Trauma

There is only one biblical book whose name is a state of the heart: Lamentations. When Jeremiah wrote it he was doing what God allows human beings to do, indeed encourages them to do: to grieve. After the trauma of being kidnapped to a strange and hostile land God's great prophet opened his heart: "Joy is gone from our hearts; our dancing has turned to mourning" (Lam. 5:15). A well-known phrase from Ecclesiastes speaks of the inevitability of grief: there is "a time to weep and a time to laugh, a time to mourn and a time to dance" (Eccles. 3:4). It is a description of a kind of life rhythm, a signal that we should not be surprised when tears come, but neither should we think that life will always be that way.

When grieving people come to pastoral counselors they want to know what God has to say to them in their pain. Pastoral counseling is, in that moment, one of the truly great opportunities, but also one of the most foreboding challenges. The opportunity is to be able to give comfort, at least a measure of comfort, to someone with a wounded heart, which is central to the historic meaning of ministry. It is the "cure of souls." Often there is no "fix" to be offered. The death has occurred; the divorce is final; the layoff is long-term. What lies ahead is an increasing awareness of the loss and the pain that accompanies it. The counselor becomes a kind of guide leading the grieving person through the pain.

One of the challenges is knowing how to proclaim and apply the love of God in unlovely situations. The counselee wants to know: where is God in all this? how could he let me be so devastated? how am I going to make it? how will I get over the loss? A cancer-stricken body is an unlovely sight, as is death itself, or the loss of a lifelong friendship. It will not help the grieving person for someone else to pretend otherwise. The pastoral counselor can provide answers to difficult questions at a time of grief, although, as we will see, there are constructive and destructive ways of providing those answers. The most profound truth is that God offers *himself* to the grieving person, and in an analogous way the pastoral counselor offers not just eloquent words, but himself or herself.

Trauma has many faces. It can happen in the split second that it takes one car to collapse another, or over years of physical abuse. It may be severe because it undermines something central to what it means to be human, for example, sexual abuse; or it may be less devastating while still influential—having major surgery or flunking a course. What is traumatic to one person may not be to another.

The pastoral counselor must be ready to help people with trauma and grief because they are not specialized and rare occurrences. They are universal and they are common. Properly dealt with trauma and grief can result in growth and maturity. Improperly handled, people can become unnecessarily stuck in their grief, alone in their trauma when they should have found comfort and fellowship.

The aim of this book is to provide those doing pastoral counseling with three things: first, a Christian, biblical understanding of trauma and grief. There are hundreds of passages of Scripture that help us understand trauma and grief and see where God has provided supernatural assistance. This is not to suggest that what the pastoral counselor needs is a few handy texts to quote and he or she can make easy work of counseling hurting people. Rather, we should seek to discover the theological network that links loss and gain, pain and healing, corruption and salvation, and offer compassionate counsel rooted in those eternal truths. Second, this book will provide psychological insights into the phenomena of trauma and grief to help the pastoral counselor anticipate and understand how different kinds of trauma will affect different people, and also understand the complex process of grieving. We also need to discern the difference between well-founded insights in these areas and popular fads. When we have grasped the points of convergence between a Christian worldview and the human experience of trauma and grief we will be more capable of giving effective, practical counsel. That is the third purpose of this book: to show how a pastoral counselor may in several sessions make a significant difference for the wounded personality. The practical examples throughout the book and the extended case study at the end are illustrations of the most common forms of trauma and grief the pastoral counselor may come across.

If it is true of Jesus himself that "a bruised reed he will not break, and a smoldering wick he will not snuff out," then it is also true that his disciples will not ignore their wounded (much less injure them further), but rather, will welcome the chance to be agents of healing.

A Definition of Grief

Grief is the natural, expected reaction to a loss. Each word in that definition is important.

1. Grief is natural. While most people do not live their lives in a constant state of grief, everyone does live through times of grief. It is not natural in the sense that we seek it, want it, or have to live constantly under its shadow, but rather in the sense that it is universal in human experience. The only way to avoid grief for a lifetime is to live in a world where there is no loss. Now some Chris-

tians will be anxious to reply that in Christ they have all sufficiency, that loss is gain, and that Christians "do not grieve like the rest of men" (1 Thess. 4:13). The Bible does say all those things, but it does not thereby say that there is no such thing as loss and the grief resulting from loss. The Scriptures talk about grief and mourning from beginning to end. They hold forth the promise that God will heal us of grief, but not bypass it. Christians do not need "to grieve like the rest of men, who have no hope," but that doesn't mean they don't grieve at all. Grief is natural because it accomplishes a constructive work in the human heart. When someone experiences the death of someone close, for instance, the painful process of grief allows the person to adjust to a world that has been changed. One has to adjust when that father isn't there anymore to ask advice of, or the wife isn't there to nurture the kids, or the job has disappeared and it's necessary to seek training for a different profession.

2. Grief is expected. Of course it is not possible to be prepared for a major loss in one's life, nor should one think that one has to be strong enough in the present moment for any possible loss or tribulation. Oftentimes God's strength and grace comes only when the need arises. On the other hand, it is a great disadvantage to be naive about life, plunging ahead fully expecting that one will always get, and keep, what one wants. That may be the case for a young person who has not had to face any significant loss, or who has always been given whatever he or she wants. Because grief is inevitable, it is better for us if we, in some sense, expect it. One of the functions of pastoral counselors and others in ministry is to contribute to building a certain worldview in the people with whom we have contact. To be honest about the reality of broken relationships, changing life circumstances, loss through disease, death, or distance—before we face them—will help us to move more quickly through grief when loss becomes reality.

3. Grief is a reaction. It is dynamic. It may begin with the internal reaction of the heart, but then there may be consequences in relationships, in life functions, and even in the grieving person's body. A teenage boy's mother dies unexpectedly. He is at first stunned, then furious, then depressed. He withdraws from his siblings and friends, and then, to medicate his pain, begins drinking excessively, which causes his depression only to get worse. Before

long he is not sleeping or eating properly, and has all but dropped out of school. There is not an area of his life that is not reacting to the awful severing of losing his mother. People who are in the middle of significant emotional, relational, and physical reactions to loss need other stable but compassionate people with whom they can connect to the degree that they are able to, and thus find a little stability themselves. The pastoral counselor is a lighthouse on the shore, a reference point, a place to look to in the midst of rapidly changing circumstances.

In another set of circumstances the reaction may be much less severe. The young mother whose first child leaves for the first time on the school bus may very well have a stabbing sense of loss. Her baby is growing up, there is no way of stopping it. It is not that she is not glad for the maturing of her little boy. But something she had before is different now. The sense of grief that first week of school will help her adapt to a new stage of life.

4. Finally, grief is the result of loss. There are the obvious losses we're all familiar with: a loved one dies, or moves away, or contracts a serious disease. Almost any kind of life issue may result in loss. You can lose money, lose your home, lose status, lose security, lose credibility. The loss may be physical, it may be relational, or it may be psychological. For instance, many people have grief reactions when they turn a certain age. For some, forty feels like the final loss of youth, for others fifty hits hard because it is like turning a corner into a later phase of life, and yet others are jarred by sixty candles on the cake because they anticipate that others will now put them in a different category. If there is the perception of loss, there will be grief. Whether the experience is simple sadness or outright mourning there is a message to listen to, a lesson to learn. Part of the constructive adaptive work of grief may be the realization that you don't really lose parts of your life, but add to them.

A Definition of Trauma

Trauma is the experience of something shocking happening to someone (physically or psychologically) that produces some kind of inner injury and affects the person's ability to function in nor-

mal ways. There are three components here: shock, injury, and function.

1. The external shock is an event that is significantly influential. Many people speak rather loosely about things they find "traumatic" in life, some of them not all that influential. "I find it traumatic going Christmas shopping," or "I found that exam traumatic," or "that movie was traumatic for me." "Traumatic" used this way is a loose way of saying something was a negative experience. Real trauma is the result of something that truly shakes someone up and has significant effects. The most common experiences resulting in trauma would be things like a severe auto accident, death of a very close person, rape, or other forms of sexual abuse, or being the victim of a crime. Most often trauma is shocking or jarring in the sense that it exerts considerable external force. Sometimes it is the unexpectedness that makes trauma so jarring. Trauma visits in its unexpected way when a person who thought he'd get to work like any normal day instead ends up in intensive care because of a heart attack, or the person who gets a call at work that his or her house is in flames, or the person who is held up at gunpoint just a block from home. Trauma is not always the result of a surprising event. The rapid progress of cancer can lead someone into several jarring stages of trauma. Each visit to the doctor and progressively worse blood count is a blow to the morale and security of the patient and his or her loved ones.

2. Trauma results in injury, a wounding of the inner life. In medicine "trauma" refers to sudden, significant injury. If you bump your head and get a headache you will take a couple of aspirin and wait an hour to see if your headache will go away, but if you fall from a ladder and hit your head on the hard ground you will be treated in a hospital emergency room for head trauma. Likewise, there are many life events that surprise us, hit us below the belt, have unpleasant consequences, but do not significantly wound us. There is no uniform list of traumatic events because different people are susceptible to inner injury to different degrees. Death of a loved one may be traumatic, but not necessarily so. In one family a middle-aged son and daughter mourn the death of their father. The daughter goes through a fairly normal grief reaction in the months after the funeral, but the son is more profoundly affected. He goes

into deep depression and can no longer function on the job. For him the death of "Dad" was traumatic because the lives of father and son, who were business partners and spent most days together, were a much closer constellation.

3. An inability to function properly is the consequence of real trauma. Physical difficulties, depression, withdrawal from relationships, irrational fears, emotional swings or emotional repression are some of the many evidences that a traumatic event or events have had damaging effects. Christians are not immune from such experiences any more than they are immune from physical disease. They have tremendous spiritual resources available to them, and the pastoral counselor has the privilege of incorporating the resources of truth, love, and fellowship into the counseling process, but they still have to face the reality that the blows and jolts of life in this world take their toll. A young mother contacts her pastor because over the past year it has become harder and harder for her to cope. Her Bible study had prayed for her on many occasions, her husband tried to take up the slack at home believing that if they held on for long enough, she would get better. Her depression and anxiety only got increasingly worse, however. When thoughts of suicide became a daily experience they both knew it was time to call out for help. The pastor was able to provide support and comfort, but because of the severity of the situation he helped get her in to see a professional counselor. Only gradually was she able to talk about the times her older brother had raped her, a secret that the whole family had guarded for fifteen years until it finally began to destroy her when she moved into a new phase of her adult life.

The Relationship between Trauma and Grief

The pastoral counselor will frequently be in the position of having to interpret the relationship between trauma and grief. A teenager is killed in an auto accident and the pastor, after getting past the painful funeral, tries to anticipate the effects on the mother and father, especially because they never get past the initial numbness until well after their son is buried. A middle-aged man comes in to see his pastor and reports that he thinks he has never really grieved the death of his father in the Korean War. A woman contacts her pastor because she feels like she has been stuck in the grief following her divorce that happened over ten years ago.

What really is the relationship between trauma and grief? All trauma will produce grief; but not all grief is the result of trauma (see Figure 1.1).

Figure 1.1

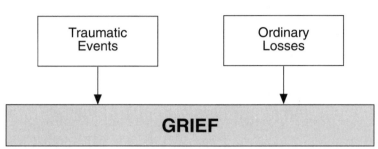

1. Trauma will produce grief. If trauma is "the experience of something shocking happening to someone that produces some kind of inner injury and affects the person's ability to function in normal ways," then naturally, all trauma is a kind of loss. Injury after a severe auto accident is the loss of physical well-being; sexual abuse is the loss of trust; unexpected death is the loss of a loved one; bankruptcy is loss of security. Grief is "the natural, expected reaction to a loss." Thus, all trauma results in some form of grief.

On the other hand there are some people for whom the natural process of grieving a loss after trauma is thwarted in some way. Perhaps the grieving is delayed for some reason, or the person going through the trauma is attempting to protect himself or herself from pain by avoiding grieving. Sooner or later there has to be an adjustment to the loss so that life can go on in a new configuration. There was one family whose son was killed with three other highschoolers in an auto accident and they thought it best to keep setting a place for him at the table, pretending as if he was still among them, to avoid the pain of their loss. They even threw him a birthday party in that first year. One of the most challenging things a pastoral counselor has to do in the area of trauma and grief is know what to say to people who, by any ordinary standards, should be adjusting their lives by sensing their loss, but refusing to do so.

2. Not all grief is the result of trauma. Trauma will ordinarily result in grief, but there are many more opportunities for us to experience grief as a part of the normal course of life. There are a multitude of losses that affect us at some level that fall short of being shocking or injurious. A friend moves across country, a family pet dies, a grandparent is moved into a nursing home, a beautiful open meadow behind the house is turned into a subdivision—such are the ordinary losses that tug at our hearts and require adjustments. We don't welcome trauma when it comes, and loss itself is not a good thing, but grief as a process of internal realignment can be something of a friend under healthy circumstances. Think about how often someone who has had a really hard cry will say that he or she feels better afterward. Instead of running away from a loss, looking it straight in the eye, feeling the sorrow or indignation or hurt, and then moving past it—the whole sweeping experience of grief—can be one of the most healing things that can happen.

Even when it comes to more minor losses, it is a good thing to be aware of and honest about a sense of loss. It doesn't mean that a person will be immobilized, or nonfunctional, or less than spiritual. He or she will be living in reality, more likely to have realistic expectations of what life offers and what it does not. Many people need to hear the simple message that it's okay to sense loss. It doesn't mean you are weak, or spoiled, or self-absorbed. It means you are living with your feet on the ground.

Issues Concerning Pastoral Counseling for Grief and Trauma

In this book we will have occasion to look at the great redemptive potential that a pastoral counselor has when dealing with grief and trauma, and the significant challenges. What follows are some of those issues.

1. How can the pastoral counselor discern the state of mind and heart of someone going through an experience of grief or trauma?

Because grief and trauma can lead someone into almost any kind of emotional state or intensity, and because those reactions vary from one person to another, it can be very tricky to discern the direction a person is heading. There may be anger, shame, fear, sadness, or hurt. Sadness can range from a slight case of the blues to deep dejection and depression. It will help the pastoral counselor to know what can be expected, and how to react.

2. How do you communicate the reality of the love of God to a person who feels and thinks that God has just dealt him or her a fatal blow?

One of the reasons a grieving person may come to a pastor in the first place is that he or she is trying to reconcile his or her belief system with tragic events that have happened. The problem of evil is a fundamental religious and philosophical issue, and is intensely personal and spiritual. People often are really looking for an answer when they ask: why did God do this to me?

3. What does the Christian gospel offer a person suffering the grief of loss or trauma?

When people seek pastoral counselors because of grief or trauma they are hoping to find some relief from their pain. They may even be seeking a way for the loss to be made up or compensated for. While pastoral counselors can provide comfort, assurance, and guidance they cannot make up for a loss that has occurred. Indeed, part of their responsibility is to reflect reality back to the counselee, to help him or her come to terms with the reality of the loss and begin the process of realigning life.

4. How can scriptural truth best be applied to a grieving person?

The Scriptures have an abundance of truths that apply to those who have experienced loss. Promises of God's love, unchangeableness, and power; truths about the nature of this world and the world to come; warnings about approaching life in unrealistic or naive ways—any of them may leap to the mind of the pastoral counselor. But he or she must carefully discern how scriptural truth will best be assimilated into the thought life and emotional life of the grieving person.

5. How do truly traumatic experiences affect a human being?

The effects of profoundly destructive actions of people on other people are well-known. Simple common sense tells us that traumatic tragedies such as rape, near-death illness, or early physical abuse will have wide-ranging effects on human personalities. But what are those effects? How can they be recognized? What difference does it make in pastoral counseling? One of the most significant issues here is how a pastoral counselor can offer something of worth to someone who is profoundly needy. When trauma results in personality disorders, for instance, what good can be accomplished with short-term counseling? There are objective indicators that a pastoral counselor can become aware of in order to discern when referral is necessary.

6. When does grieving end?

To put it in other words: Are there appropriate limits to grieving? Does the grieving person have control over grief? Should he or she? There is a constructive purpose to grieving: to make adjustments to a new situation necessitated because a loss has occurred. The desired outcome, of course, is for the grieving person to do the work of grief and to go on with life. That does not preclude, however, the periodic stabbing pains of regret or sorrow that may come at any time in the future: for instance, when someone recalls the memory of someone close who has died. The pastoral counselor wants the counselee to experience healing after loss, but must avoid the temptation to force the outcome.

7. What stands in the way of grief?

Those who choose a path of avoiding grief may simply buy for themselves much more complicated problems later on. It is human nature to want to run from pain, and a little bad theology that says that there is never sadness in the life of the faithful can only amplify that tendency. There are many things that can stand in the way of grief besides human nature and bad theology: uncomfortable friends and acquaintances who almost require the grieving person to slap on a smile; roles that the person has adopted in life that dictate that he or she had better not be weak for a moment (more bad theology); lack of good models of grieving. The pastoral counselor is not just helping a grieving person work through grief, but is providing a model for grieving for the audience always attracted by the tragedy of loss.

8. Where does Christian hope affect the grief experience?

Paul says that Christians do not grieve like the rest of humanity, which has no hope. To put it simply: hope makes a difference. But what is that hope? How does eternal hope become a source of strength in this troubled world? What is the role of hope in this life? Can the pastoral counselor hold out the belief and the hope that mourning will come to an end? What about the hope that someone holds onto for a father recovering from a heart attack, or hope for a teenager who is destroying himself with drugs; or hope for a mother whose grief has brought about a two-year depression? Even medical health professionals acknowledge the importance of the spiritual condition we call hope. The pastoral counselor has the privilege and responsibility to offer both compassion and hope to grieving and traumatized people.

9. Is trauma objective or subjective?

It would be easier for any counselor if trauma were a purely objective phenomenon. We could rank or measure how "bad" a certain experience was and then determine an appropriate response. The reality, however, is that while there are certain events that we can assume are traumatic to almost anybody, there are other experiences that may be traumatic to one person but not another. The same is true even for physical trauma. A fall on the sidewalk may be an almost daily experience for a small child, but can mark the beginning of the end for an elderly person.

10. Is grieving a cognitive (intellectual) or affective (emotional) experience, or both?

One school of thought would say that beliefs (thoughts) are the wellspring of human experience whereas another would say that feelings have a life of their own and have to be handled directly, apart from cognitive processes. These two paradigms (affect primacy or cognition primacy) will produce differing approaches to grieving and traumatized persons, and they are not the only possible paradigms. It will be important, therefore, before we proceed, to lay down a framework of how thought and emotion work together in the spiritual life of an individual.

Thought, Emotion, and the Spiritual Life

When pastoral counselors help people with grief or trauma they are dealing with issues of the innermost heart of human experience. These spiritual issues arouse both mind and heart, thought and emotion. Grief and trauma are issues of thought and emotion because they are the junctures of life where belief systems cross over highly emotionally charged experiences including fear, anger, shame, and sorrow. The pastoral counselor will deal with such questions as: Why am I angry at my brother for dying? How does God look at my sorrow? Why don't the things I believe intellectually make a difference in my heart? Does my sadness mean I've lost my faith? When am I going to feel close to God again?

The Scriptures have a whole range of descriptions of how the inner life of a person functions. "Mind" emphasizes the rational capabilities, "will," the volitional. "Heart" includes the emotions, although it also is used to describe the whole inner person. "Soul" means we are animated, living creatures, and "spirit," that we are related to God. Taken together the terms do not describe the different rooms of a house or the parts of some intangible anatomy. Rather, they describe the way we as whole, unified creatures function in our inner lives.

It is common in psychological terms to distinguish between the rational, thinking part of the self and the emotional side. Cognition and affect are two kinds of responses to external stimuli. As God-designed capabilities they help us know how best to respond to the changing circumstances around us.

Thought is the active mental function whereby we process information and draw conclusions. Thought allows us to make interpretations of life, predict what will happen, and evaluate the best way to respond. It is the way our inner selves give structure to the course of our lives. Christians seek to have "the mind of Christ" in the sense of adopting the rational perception of life that he offers on the basis of his truth.

When things are going well (i.e., when there is no trauma or grief to deal with) a person has a certain way of thinking about life. This belief system, philosophy or theology of life, determines expectations and aspirations. We observe others going through trauma or grief and—if we are thinking at all—we will incorporate those observations into our worldview.

Then trauma or grief hits closer to home. Our minds react by sorting out new information coming quickly at us. And we respond emotionally, in the case of real trauma or significant loss causing grief, perhaps with a surge of emotions. The question then becomes: have we developed enough of a belief system, philosophy, or theology of life to weather the storm of emotions coming our way? C. S. Lewis said he was "surprised by joy," but according to the opening words of his *A Grief Observed*, written in the aftermath of the death of his wife, it appears that he was also surprised by the surges of grief: "No one ever told me that grief felt so like fear. I am not afraid, but the sensation is like being afraid. The same fluttering in the stomach, the same restlessness, the yawning. I keep on swallowing" (p. 1).

We might compare emotions to weather. Ask a meteorologist whether there will be any weather today and he'll respond that there is always weather. It may be wet or dry, mild or severe, safe or dangerous—but there's always weather. We were created by God with an affective side that is never turned off. At any particular moment the predominant emotion may be joy or sadness, compassion or anger, fear or peace. While different people may be subtly or strongly emotional, there is no such thing as a person without emotion.

Such a state would be a tragedy because there is a God-designed purposefulness to emotion. Like the nerve tissues of the body, emotions signal what is going on in the exterior world so that we will better know how to react. The emotion of joy tells us that something seems right, fear warns of danger or threat, anger says there is something wrong or unjust somewhere, hurt says there is something injurious happening, and sadness is the signal that some loss has occurred. An important qualification needs to be added at this point: though this is the way our emotions are to function ideally, they are far from infallible and for many different reasons may not be accurate measurements of what is objectively going on in the world around us. This is, of course, consistent with the truth that we are fallen creatures, that all of us, and all of the ways in which we function, are affected by the inherent corruptibility of the human condition.

Some Christians have been taught not only that emotions are inherently untrustworthy, but that they should be ignored or shunned in favor of the supposed "higher" functions of the soul (and some assert this point with great emotion!). This is an overreaction to the possible pitfalls of the subjectivity of emotions. Discipleship does not mean the suppression of affective experience, but rather, bringing the whole self—including cognition and affect—under the lordship of Christ so that both function better as interpreters and processors of truth. After all, what else was Jesus modeling when he showed his compassion, sorrow, anger, joy, and even fear, always as accurate and appropriate reactions to what was going on around him. The quelling of emotion is not the pathway to righteousness but to rationalism. It is as unsatisfactory a solution as any other that attempts to deal with the infirmities, frailties, or shortcomings of any human function by suppressing it— the ascetic's way of dealing with the body, or the mystic's way of surpassing the mind. It will not do to deify emotion so that subjective experience is the point of living, but neither will it do to deify intellect in a way that assumes that our rational processes are always accurate and righteous.

Trauma and grief are almost always occasions when belief systems are tested and emotions are stretched to the limit. They are events of great inner activity, times when links to God and links to the truth may become weaker or stronger, depending upon how the trauma or grief is dealt with. A pastoral counselor dealing with a traumatized or grieving person is in the privileged and highly responsible role of helping someone through this complex network of thoughts and feelings. It is a journey of the soul previously charted by the protagonists in some of the greatest stories of the Scriptures: Joseph, Job, David, Jeremiah, Paul, and even Jesus. It is the prelude to blessedness as defined by the Lord himself: "Blessed are those who mourn, for they will be comforted" (Matt. 5:4).

2

Grief, Trauma,
and a Biblical Worldview

Biblical Perspectives

The biblical story begins with the gain of creation, moves quickly to the loss of the fall, and continues through the Old Testament and New with the message of how a damaged world continues to experience loss and how God's salvation offers healing. This cosmic cycle of gain, loss, and restoration—and with them grief and trauma—is repeated in the personal lives of all human beings including all the major stories and characters of the Bible. The Bible is a book about grief and trauma. The pastoral counselor can thus offer compassion and support that has a broad and strong foundation of biblical truth. Many of the biblical texts commented on in this chapter may be the best passages a Christian pastoral counselor can offer someone in the crisis of trauma or grief.

There are many reasons why the Christian counselor can offer a better and deeper ministry of counsel than someone with no Christian faith. A biblical worldview includes an understanding of loss, sin, tragedy, and wickedness. It holds forth the hope that there is restoration beyond loss, and that God can take the rubble of life

43

and build new things from it. And, perhaps most important, it describes the unchangeable presence of God in and through grief and trauma. Available to the Christian counselor is not just a handful of biblical verses to toss the way of the counselee occasionally, but rather a whole outlook on life—this life and the life beyond—that has historically enabled Christians to find forms of restoration that surpass all other attempts.

After considering the general perspectives that the Bible offers on trauma and grief we will move on to the immense and sometimes foreboding question "Why?"; then look at the love of God in a suffering world; and finally a biblical view of the healing process of grief.

Grief and the Ordinary Life

It is popular to quote the promises of God in the Scriptures unless they are like the statement of Jesus in John 16:33: "In this world you will have trouble." Such expressions are always accompanied by a word of encouragement and hope, of course, but we should not thereby ignore the harder part of the truth. Psalm 90:10 is brutally honest: "The length of our days is seventy years—or eighty, if we have the strength; yet their span is but trouble and sorrow, for they quickly pass, and we fly away." Such expressions are not the whole truth, but they are part of the truth.

The Scriptures assume that the "trouble" that comes in this world will impact even the strongest of God's servants. The Bible's pages are drenched in places with tears. From the story of Joseph in Genesis to Job, Psalms, Proverbs, Lamentations, and even Jesus at the tomb of Lazarus and in the Garden of Gethsemane, we find that in the course of life losses will occur and losses will hurt. "Even in laughter the heart may ache, and joy may end in grief" says Proverbs 14:13, which tells us immediately that the solution to the problem of loss in a fallen world is not the avoidance of grief, but coming through it, and being strengthened because of it.

The more one knows about life, the more one will be familiar with grief. That seems to be the point of Ecclesiastes 1:18: "for with much wisdom comes much sorrow; the more knowledge, the more grief." Year by year our personal experience of life, like an enlarging circle, encompasses more of its joys and more of its sorrows. Ask people what they understand about life today more than they did ten years ago and you will find that their cumulative experiences of loss have presented many opportunities to grieve. Of course people can in a self-protective way erect all kinds of barriers in an attempt to isolate themselves from the sting of loss and thus they will not have deepened their understanding of life. There are also plenty of people who have gone through cycles of loss and grief but have not had the ability to reflect on it all and incorporate it into an attitude and philosophy of life. Far better when sorrow can produce a deeper wisdom. The pastoral counselor is in a position to provide both comfort and wisdom. The spiritual learning that can happen during times of grief is that constructive work that will help a person the next time loss comes expectedly or unexpectedly knocking.

Entering the "House of Mourning"

In the New International Version of the Bible the words mourning and sorrow appear 174 times. We are familiar with some of the rituals of mourning we see in Semitic culture like sackcloth and ashes and other foreign-looking customs. These rites of grief served a constructive purpose: to help a person come to terms with the reality of a loss, accept the loss, and make life adjustments in order to move on.

The book of Ecclesiastes makes some people nervous because of its dark, seemingly pessimistic view of life. It is, of course, one portion of biblical revelation that must be read in the context of the whole. It shows in vivid terms the effects of loss in the human experience, a lesson in why we so desperately need a transcendent God to make sense of life. One of the most poignant biblical passages about mourning occurs in this book:

> It is better to go to a house of mourning than to go to a house of feasting, for death is the destiny of every man; the living should take this to heart. Sorrow is better than laughter, because a sad face is good for the heart. The heart of the wise is in the house of mourning, but the heart of fools is in the house of pleasure (Eccles. 7:2–4).

The "house of mourning" serves well as a metaphor for the whole process of grief that is inevitable in the face of significant loss. Grieving is a subset of our normal experience, a parenthetical time when our inner lives are attempting to adjust to the seemingly rude and jarring experience of loss.

The writer of Ecclesiastes speaks of the inevitability of grief ("death is the destiny of every man"), but beyond that, places a certain value on it: "it is better to go to a house of mourning . . ." The meaning is not that grief is inherently better than joy, but that when external circumstances are painful, distressing, or traumatic, when a person is really injured inside, it is best to be truthful and honest both to oneself and to others about it, mourn the loss, rather than paste on an artificial and fragile smile. We have all met people who feel a certain obligation to be joyful at all times; it may come from a certain affective "orthodoxy" that they were taught by the church that was most formative in their lives. Or it may have come from family members who preferred not to be made uncomfortable by anybody's sadness, so the rule of the house was: if you're hurting, keep it to yourself.

But Ecclesiastes says "a sad face is good for the heart," a proverb that surely spoils the social expectations of many a relationship, family, or church. But why? What possible benefits are there from the external expression of mourning? Two reasons stand out: first, a harmony of inner and outer experiences—simple truthfulness—always works in our best interest. It takes a lot of work to force a fake laugh, to paste on a superficial smile. A person who goes through the funeral of a loved one suppressing every tear, strangling every moan may very well end up with more spiritual and emotional pain rather than less. "Sorrow is better than laughter."

Another reason why "a sad face is good for the heart" is that the shape of the human visage is one of the most important God-designed means of social communication. A happy face invites others to share the joy, an angry face warns, a fearful face is a call for assistance, and a sad face says: I'm injured, I'm weakened right now, you may not be able to have normal expectations of me, I may need your understanding and help. All those facial muscles work together to send out signals that help us reflect to those around us the reality of our situations. A sad face is good when by any normal standards a person enters grievous circumstances.

One other extremely important point must be made. Mourning is not lack of faith. It is true that faith can inspire joy, that there is a Christian hope that elevates us beyond the tragic twists and turns of life, and that Christ said "your grief will turn to joy" (John 16:20). But none of that should be translated into "faithful Christians do not mourn." One can be in the house of mourning and still be full of faith. In fact, it can be argued that the most basic, substantive faith is found in those who are in the middle of their mourning. Job and David (in the Psalms) frequently speak sorrowfully and even angrily to God and then speak of ultimate faith in the goodness of God. The very act of communicating with God in times of distress is a demonstration of faith.

The house of mourning is not a permanent residence. Some grief may be long-term; there are some forms of regret that will come up whenever a distant memory is revived. But the hard work of mourning, under ordinary circumstances, is something we move into for a season, and then out. No one can say exactly how long grief lasts—it depends on the kind of loss and the kind of person. There was one church where the standard teaching was that mourning could last for three months, but then it should be over. That convenient conclusion (i.e., convenient to those who felt put out by the sadness of others) was drawn from 1 Peter 1:6, which speaks of grieving "for a season," one more reminder that if we try hard enough we can get the Bible to say whatever we want it to say.

Rituals of Grief

Whereas grieving has become culturally neat and tidy in our times, in the biblical world we find very deliberate rituals whose function it was to reflect the reality of loss back to the mourners, and to mark a passage (or the beginning of passage) through the grief. Wearing sackcloth and covering oneself with ashes was not merely an act of self-debasement. The rough, scratchy sackcloth was an external attire that matched the inner discomfort of loss; the ashes that dirtied the body were an external reminder of loss, and again, helped to bring the outer person into harmony with the inner person. Other rituals of mourning in the Old Testament include fasting, the rending of garments, the plucking of beard and hair, walking barefoot, covering the face and head, neglecting personal appearance, sitting on the ground, and wearing mourning dress.

We have some small vestige of that kind of tradition in the wearing of black clothing at a funeral. Some decades back it was common for a widow to wear black for a full year after the death of her spouse. To some today that notion appears morose, but there was one woman who said she wished the custom still prevailed. Two weeks after the death of her husband she brought her son's bicycle into a bike shop for a flat tire to be fixed. When the store owner said (in a way that he thought was being helpful), "Doing this isn't so hard. You should have your old man do it," the widow was stunned. She knew she couldn't resent what the man had said, after all, how could he know? Yet his very ignorance hurt. Looking back on the incident much later she remarked: "I wish widows still wore black."

When the Jews of Esther's time heard an edict of persecution they entered a kind of class mourning: "In every province to which the edict and order of the king came, there was great mourning among the Jews, with fasting, weeping and wailing. Many lay in sackcloth and ashes" (Esth. 4:3). When Jacob was told that Joseph had been killed by a wild animal he "tore his clothes, put on sackcloth and mourned for his son many days. All his sons and daughters came to comfort him, but he refused to be comforted. 'No,' he said, 'in mourning will I go down to the grave to my son.' So his father wept for him" (Gen. 37:34–35). It is actually Joseph who eventually mourned the death of Jacob in a poignant scene in the last chapter of Genesis:

> When they reached the threshing floor of Atad, near the Jordan, they lamented loudly and bitterly; and there Joseph observed a seven-day period of mourning for his father. When the Canaanites who lived there saw the mourning at the threshing floor of Atad, they said, "The Egyptians are holding a solemn ceremony of mourning." That is why that place near the Jordan is called Abel Mizraim (Gen. 50:10–11).

Mourning is here described as "solemn" and a "ceremony." Cultural anthropologists study the widely divergent rituals of death—the ceremonies—that are adopted by different cultures in order to mark the passage from death to life. While the ceremony may concentrate on the deceased, its purpose extends to the living.

The whole point of ceremony is to in a deliberate and public way mark an important life event. Ceremonies of death help to make the loss real to those who remain. Funerals are not easy, but they serve to drive home the reality of the death of the loved one. The "visitation" that occurs in a funeral home very often the day before a funeral can be the hardest part of all. The casket may be open, family and friends file by, struck by the stillness and finality of death, the last chance to see the deceased. Sometimes it is a calm scene, but sometimes heartwrenching, even emotionally violent. Yet somehow the funeral the next day seems easier. Life looks different later, but adaptable.

Ceremony also validates and ennobles important life events. Weddings, graduations, and even birthday parties do that for the happy occasions, but even death ceremonies play a positive role. The ceremony of mourning is a way of saying, "death is part of life, we are not surprised by it, we recognize it, we even accept it." Over the years we go to more and more funerals, the similarities between them further confirming the normalcy of loss in life.

A ceremony of mourning will also be an affirmation of the positive value of life—death does not invalidate life. In a Christian funeral there will be words of eternal life in Scripture, testimony, or sermon. The common gathering of family and friends for a meal at the conclusion of the ceremony usually turns out to be one more (frequently unconscious) affirmation of life: fellowship and food are life-giving.

The Egyptian rite marking the death of Jacob is called a "solemn" ceremony. The earnestness, seriousness, and sobriety of the rituals of mourning are a stark contrast with the superficiality and shallowness that is all too often the life posture of people in the modern world. One expects animals to live at the level of appetite and visceral drives, and then, when death happens, it just happens. But with human beings death is a cosmic moment, a time for earnest reflection, an opportunity for creatures of rationality and moral purpose to be able to reexamine their priorities, relationships, and lifestyle. It is a philosophical event, even though waves of powerful emotion may be the first level of experience.

Biblical culture recognized all this. Modern Western culture on the other hand is mixed. Many individuals have a hard time knowing what to do with the losses of life like death, because they don't know what to do with life itself. The church can be and should be different. The pastoral counselor is the speaking guide, helping the person experiencing loss to note the landscape of their time of mourning—to be able to see life from a different but fuller perspective and be more ready to move on.

Scenes of Trauma

Because of the honesty of the revealed word of God we find many examples of the terrible, traumatic experiences that are possible in a fallen world. We will look at two specific cases: the rape of Tamar and the trials of Job.

The Rape of Tamar

A scandal in a prominent political family, rape, incest, cover-up, revenge by murder: all the makings of a modern novel perhaps, but also one chapter in the Scriptures. Second Samuel 13, which details the story of the rape of Tamar, is one of those biblical chapters that is hard to read much less explain. Yet here is the proof that the Bible gives no Pollyanna perspective on life, but instead uncovers and addresses the greatest struggles human beings face.

It all happened in the royal family. Amnon, the son of King David, developed a lust for his own half-sister, Tamar, a beautiful young woman. As his desire became near obsessive he plotted her seduction. He arranged for her to deliver him food in his bedroom and tried to entice her: "Come to bed with me, my sister." She resisted and the violent act resulted:

[12] "Don't, my brother!" she said to him. "Don't force me. Such a thing should not be done in Israel! Don't do this wicked thing. [13] What about me? Where could I get rid of my disgrace? And what about you? You would be like one of the wicked fools in Israel. Please

speak to the king; he will not keep me from being married to you."
[14] But he refused to listen to her, and since he was stronger than she,
he raped her. [15] Then Amnon hated her with intense hatred. In fact,
he hated her more than he had loved her. Amnon said to her, "Get
up and get out!" [16] "No!" she said to him. "Sending me away would
be a greater wrong than what you have already done to me." But he
refused to listen to her. [17] He called his personal servant and said,
"Get this woman out of here and bolt the door after her." [18] So his
servant put her out and bolted the door after her. She was wearing
a richly ornamented robe, for this was the kind of garment the virgin daughters of the king wore. [19] Tamar put ashes on her head and
tore the ornamented robe she was wearing. She put her hand on her
head and went away, weeping aloud as she went.

Using the previously discussed definition of trauma ("the experience of something shocking happening to someone that produces some kind of inner injury and affects the person's ability
to function in normal ways"), it is not hard to find each of these
three elements.

Rape is always shocking because it is, by definition, an unwel-
come intrusion, an unexpected attack. This story has an especially
sinister character because of the premeditation of Amnon, and his
extreme rejection after he inflicted pain. The shock was physical,
psychological, and social.

The inner injury of Tamar is immediately evidenced in her reaction, the tearing of her richly ornamented royal robe, putting ashes
on her head, walking about hand on head, weeping aloud: a beautiful virgin turned into a visage of destitution. The tragic outcome
of it all is indicated in a single phrase: "and Tamar lived in her
brother Absalom's house, a desolate woman."

Thus Tamar's "ability to function in normal ways" was affected
in the extreme. Yet one of the most important lessons of this difficult story is how the trauma experienced by Tamar affected not
just her but a whole family constellation; indeed, it may be argued,
an entire nation. King David's reaction when he heard of the incident was to be furious (2 Sam. 13:21), yet there is no indication that
the king did anything except ignore the situation. Tamar's brother
Absalom's anger turned to bitter hatred. He "never said a word to
Amnon, either good or bad; he hated Amnon because he had dis-

graced his sister Tamar" (13:22). Passive anger became intense hostility and animosity that two years later turned violent when Absalom carried out his plot to kill Amnon in the remote hill country. Again there is the tearing of robes and bitter tears in the royal palace (13:31, 36) resulting in a five-year estrangement between David and Absalom. In the last two years Absalom lived in the small city of David itself, he and the king avoiding each other. Absalom named his own daughter Tamar. He eventually took the reigns of power from his father in a political coup, only to lose his own life in the brief civil war that followed.

Trauma heaped on trauma. It would be a stretch to say that the rape of Tamar was the cause of the pain and devastation that would affect all of Israel during those years, but by the same token we should note that it marks the beginning of the disintegration of a whole family. Trauma is injury. If not dealt with properly, without the opportunity for healing, not only is the traumatized person unable to regain social relationships, a sense of well-being, and an ability to function normally, but many others may settle into maladaptive behaviors.

The Trials of Job

Job is not an easy book to read. If we can read it casually we might best check to see if we have shut off our normal sensitivities. It is an extended picture of trauma, a case of faith being fired in the crucible of a painful, fallen world. Here again the Scriptures provide an anatomy of trauma.

His losses are stark in contrast with his previous prosperity and health. He was "blameless and upright; he feared God and shunned evil." He was a man of power and stature: "the greatest man among all the people of the East." The story of Job is an extended illustration of that principle enunciated by Jesus: God "causes his sun to rise on the evil and the good, and sends rain on the righteous and the unrighteous."

Job's trauma and loss were extreme and diverse. He lost his wealth and servants to raiders (1:13, 16, 17), his sons and daughters to natural catastrophe (1:18), and his physical well-being to debilitating disease (2:7). It is hardly fair to read the remaining forty chapters of the book of Job without stopping and considering what those kinds of losses would feel like. It certainly comes as no surprise that Job lashes out at those around him, interrogates God, and even contemplates suicide.

Job's reaction to the initial losses of family and wealth was to take the posture of mourning: "Job got up and tore his robe and shaved his head," and to try to hold onto God: "The Lord gave and the Lord has taken away, may the name of the Lord be praised." The writer comments: "In all this, Job did not sin by charging God with wrongdoing" (1:20–22).

The trauma intensifies, however, when Job contracts a terrible disease. He uses pieces of broken pottery to scrape the sores that developed from his soles to the top of his head. Trauma can disrupt relationships, and in the case of Job's wife, it brought out the worst: "Are you still holding on to your integrity? Curse God and die!" Though Job would later deal with spiritual stress, pain, and even bitterness, he rejects the proposition that it would be better to abandon God: "You are talking like a foolish woman. Shall we accept good from God, and not trouble?" Part of integrity is having a certain stable view of the structure of life. Prior to his own trials Job knew that life can be full of goodness and full of trouble. That worldview is what prevents him from abandoning all that he had believed and had stood for before his own troubles.

Most of the book of Job is an intense exchange between Job and three friends. Trauma is a relational experience. Hurting people draw the attention of others. Some are sympathetic, some are horrified, some are indifferent. The hurting person stands out because we all wonder when suffering might come our way. What will it be? What will it feel like? How will I react? Will others reject me?

Suffering draws attention; it also invites interpretation. The judgmental stance of Job's friends is not an exceptional reaction. When someone lands in the hospital, for instance, almost everyone visiting will be looking for an interpretation: why is he sick? has he been working too hard, eating the wrong foods? why didn't his doctor see this coming? When someone winds up in ICU following an auto accident the questions are endless: how did it happen? why didn't he see the other car? was he sleepy because he was driving so late at night? why doesn't he listen to the advice of his friends who have told him he shouldn't drive so late? When things go wrong in life, our instinct is to try to assign blame. Perhaps we think that if we can put our finger on someone or something that is to blame, then we feel less vulnerable to the unexpected visitation of tragedy in our own lives. A biblical worldview, however, says that oftentimes bad things happen just because the world is in a state of decay. No matter how many equations we think we have figured out as to what causes injury, there is still the possibility that loss can occur at any time to anyone simply because he or she lives in a fallen world.

Job's friends examined him from every possible angle. What have you done, Job? What is your attitude toward God? Don't you think you're a bit arrogant for not coming up with an explanation yourself? All of which raises an important question for the pastoral counselor: what is the role of interpretation in ministering to grieving and traumatized persons? The inference of the book of Job is that what his friends did was not the way to do it. What is not in the story is what might have happened if Job's friends had taken a more sympathetic and supportive role. Here is a man who was truly traumatized. He is asking himself "why" questions, but he needs more than that. His main question is: has God abandoned me? Am I spiritually alone? Has my connection with my God been severed forever? What Job's friends could have done—what any pastoral counselor can do—is to testify to the ongoing, unchanging presence of God, in part, by showing a personal presence. If biblical theology indicated that for every specific malady that befalls a human being there is a specific sin causing it—which it does not—then dealing with a traumatized person may be like diagnosing car problems.

The very fact that the book of Job is in the biblical canon says that God wants us to understand that trauma and loss can happen to anybody (even the most righteous), and that when it does happen its effects are felt in all relationships, and that the only real refuge at such times is faith in the reality and goodness of God. There are many other scenes of trauma in the Scriptures: the betrayal of Joseph, the persecution of Jeremiah, the martyrdom of Stephen, the incarceration of Paul to name just a few. A biblical view of the way life works serves to lessen the element of surprise. The Bible is the most honest book one will ever find. The hope it offers is not a minimizing of pain and loss, or the naive wishful thinking of people with warm and vague religious sentiment. It is the story of salvation, in the face of the real losses that people in the modern world face every day.

The Biggest Question: Why?

It's one of the hardest questions, if not the hardest question, that anyone can be asked by someone suffering—why is this happening to me? It's a part of what philosophers call the problem of evil. The question, from a theological point of view, raises issues across every major category of theology: the nature of God (is he good? is he just? is he omnipotent?), the nature of man (is he deserving?), sin (what are its consequences?), salvation (what kind of deliverance can be expected?), and eschatology (is death an enemy or a friend? what kind of relief does the life beyond hold? is any of that relief to be experienced in this life?).

What's behind the "Why"?

As we proceed we will assume two things: 1) the "why" question is inevitable and deserves a thoughtful answer; but 2) the person going through grief or trauma needs more than an answer. The Bible does provide explanations of why there is suffering and loss in the world, but it also offers the overwhelming reality of the love and presence of God to the sufferers. When the pastoral counselor is asked "why is this happening to me?" the first step must be trying to understand what's behind the why. There are radically different scenarios. The person who is asking the question as he or she contemplates a loss that happened years ago may very well be trying to fill in or repair his or her faith. "Why?" is a nagging question, and it's time to seek some answers. Then again, when a pastoral counselor hears the question from someone who has just experienced loss or tragedy, someone who is in the midst of the surging waves of emotion, an intellectually tidy answer will not "solve" the "problem" of the pain. Indeed, one of the greatest mistakes a pastoral counselor can make is to see the pain as a problem to be solved. Injury requires healing, not definition.

We will address this issue of approaching the pain-filled counselee in subsequent chapters, but to further pursue the purpose of the present chapter, we do need to describe the answer that a biblical worldview gives to this question.

Why, O Lord?

[1] Why, O LORD, do you stand far off? Why do you hide yourself in times of trouble? [2] In his arrogance the wicked man hunts down the weak, who are caught in the schemes he devises. . . . [11] He says to himself, "God has forgotten; he covers his face and never sees." [12] Arise, LORD! Lift up your hand, O God. Do not forget the helpless. [13] Why does the wicked man revile God? Why does he say to himself, "He won't call me to account"? [14] *But you, O God, do see trouble and grief*; you consider it to take it in hand. *The victim commits himself to you*; you are the helper of the fatherless. [15] Break the arm of the wicked and evil man; call him to account for his wickedness that would not be found out. [16] The LORD is King for ever and ever; the nations will perish from his land. [17] *You hear*, O LORD, the desire of the afflicted; you encourage them, and *you listen* to their cry, [18] defending the fatherless and the oppressed, in order that man, who is of the earth, may terrify no more (Ps. 10; italics added).

The question is inevitable. If not "why?" it may be "how long?" "How long must I wrestle with my thoughts and every day have sorrow in my heart? How long will my enemy triumph over me?" (Ps. 13:2). Every religion in the world is founded on the premise that there is something right in the world, and something wrong—but how can that be? And how can I derive the good instead of the bad.

When pain and loss become my neighbors, it seems like God is far away ("why . . . do you stand far off?"), or it seems like God doesn't care ("why do you hide yourself?"). By the way most counselees talk, they seem to know the difference between objective reality and subjective experience. Rarely will a professed believer announce to the pastoral counselor that God has indeed abandoned the world he created. More often he or she will say: "I don't feel close to God," or "why is he letting this happen?" or "why doesn't he help me?"—all sentiments not far removed from Psalm 10 and a score of other passages like it.

Comfort begins with knowing that God knows: "you, O God, do see trouble and grief." This belief is not necessarily the end of questioning, the retort sometimes being: "If he does know, then why doesn't he do something?" But that retort is not always the next thing on the lips of the suffering person. There is consolation in knowing that God knows, knowing that he is present. If the pastoral counselor worries that that is not enough to offer, he or she should consider this: in the myriad places the Bible raises the question of "why?" the truth that is the greatest refuge is the ongoing presence of God. Whether one looks at the troubled life of Abraham, Joseph, Moses, Job, David, Jeremiah, Stephen, Paul, or John one finds the comfort of God coming in the conviction that we do not live our lives isolated from the goodness and power of God even when we are tasting the bitter gall of persecution, illness, or other loss. If we decide to believe that God is not present, our pain would be no easier to deal with.

God "sees trouble and grief," he "considers it, and takes it in hand," he "listens to the cry . . . of the oppressed." There is no enemy of humanity that God will not, one day, put in its place. The victim will be vindicated, which is why "the victim commits himself" to God.

Romans 8 and the Nature of a Fallen World

Insofar as there are universal principles at work in humanity as a whole, the meaning of individual experience needs to be interpreted in the light of those principles. The deeply felt personal questions of our lives are, not surprisingly, couched in subjective terms: why did my mother have to die? why is my body so feeble? why did I have to lose my job? Personal experience is a real and valid part of the collective experience of humanity, but meaning more often comes from the top down, from the universal to the personal.

That is the import of a passage like Romans 8, a text of Scripture that many Christian pastoral counselors will say they refer to more than any other passage, and that not simply because it has such uplifting expressions as: "we know that in all things God works for the good of those who love him" and "if God is for us, who can be against us?" and "who shall separate us from the love of Christ?" but also because it gives an honest assessment of why bad things happen, truths about the bondage, decay, and frustration of creation.

> [18]I consider that our *present sufferings* are not worth comparing with the *glory* that will be revealed in us. [19]The creation waits in eager expectation for the sons of God to be revealed. [20]For the creation was *subjected to frustration*, not by its own choice, but by the will of the one who subjected it, in hope [21]that the creation itself will be liberated from its *bondage to decay* and brought into the glorious freedom of the children of God. [22]We know that the whole creation has been *groaning as in the pains of childbirth* right up to the present time. [23]Not only so, but we ourselves, who have the firstfruits of the Spirit, *groan inwardly* as we *wait eagerly* for our adoption as sons, the *redemption* of our bodies. [24]For in this *hope* we were saved. But hope that is seen is no hope at all. Who hopes for what he already has? [25]But if we hope for what we do not yet have, we wait for it patiently. [26]In the same way, the Spirit helps us in our *weakness* (italics added).

This incredible passage brings our perspective back to the whole of creation and pictures it in a state of pain and grief. One of the issues that commentators debate is whether or not "creation" in this passage includes mankind. Either way, by verse 23 Paul is talking about us, and surely the point of the passage is to put our sufferings in the broader context of the pain and distress of the whole created order. Thus, if I experience heart-wrenching losses in my life, it is because the whole world has become a place where losses occur in the ordinary course of things. There are three ideas repeated throughout this passage: the reality of suffering, the way suffering is experienced, and hope that extends beyond suffering.

The Reality of Loss	The Experience of Frustration	The Hope for Something Better
"present sufferings"	"subjected to frustration"	"eager expectation"
"bondage to decay"	"groaning"	"in hope"
"pains of childbirth"	"groan inwardly"	"we wait eagerly"

Is this not a picture of any person experiencing grief? What Paul here calls "frustration" and "groaning" may translate in our experience into sadness, crying, depression, anger, or rage. Loss comes as an insult or an external assault. It hurts, it injures. It is an "inward groaning" because the frustration occurs at the center of our inner lives. Grief is indeed a kind of spiritual crisis. Beyond emotion and beyond intellectual questioning, it is the sense of disjunction or displacement in our souls—the sense that "this is not the way things are supposed to be." As one commentator puts it, "frustration" is "the disappointing character of present existence, which nowhere reaches the perfection of which it is capable" (Everett, Harrison, *Expositor's Bible Commentary*, vol. 10, p. 94). "Frustration," which also has the sense of "futility" is why we ask "why?"

This frustration is the consequence of the reality of loss in the world we inhabit. The phrase "present sufferings" is literally "the sufferings of the present time"; in other words, suffering is part of the character of this whole age. It is a fundamental characteristic of life as we know it. From Genesis to Revelation the Scriptures in every way help us not to be surprised when we encounter pain or loss in this age. Genesis 3 speaks of toil and pain, thorns, thistles, enmity, and death; Revelation's cycles of seals, trumpets, and bowls depict the ever increasing patterns of war, famine, and natural catastrophe just before the final redemption.

The bare honesty of the issue is that this world is in "bondage to decay." "Decay" is the quality of corruptibility, of perishability. Paul uses the same word in 1 Corinthians 15 when comparing the eternal, permanent, and perfect nature of the resurrection body to the bodies we now possess.

Yet why do so many people still seem surprised when they get sick and die? Sometimes this happens to people who have lived a good number of years with extraordinary peace, prosperity, and health. They simply have not had anything bad happen to them or to anyone close to them, and so, when the doctor brings news of a chronic and debilitating disease to a 35-year-old, the patient is cast into confusion because he is presented with a situation entirely out of his experience. Indeed, in the post-World War II generations we have whole classes of people who have never seen war, famine, or economic devastation, which means that there will continue to be many individuals shocked and scandalized when they first have contact with the "decay" that is the "bondage" of this life.

Another reason people seem surprised by suffering is that it is, and always will be, a contradiction of what seems good and right. In Romans 8 Paul is offering a sympathetic perspective on suffering. By calling it frustration, decay, and bondage he is, in a sense, giving us permission to be frustrated and insulted. Jesus was indignant and hurt by the insult of the death of his friend Lazarus. It will not do anyone any good to try to pretend that pain doesn't hurt. Pastoral counseling that attempts to minimize the pain of trauma and loss is fundamentally dishonest. It is an illicit shortcut to reconciliation and healing.

One final observation about this portion of Romans 8: one of the ways to cope in a world of frustration is hope. The phrase "eager expectation" pictures a person "leaning forward out of intense interest and desire" (Sanday & Headlam, p. 94). Paul also says "we wait eagerly" for future redemption; and that, if we have hope, we will wait for complete healing "patiently." This is an eschatological truth, and, like all such truth, when properly apprehended, it has a present-day effect. Pastoral counseling cannot ignore the future any more than it can ignore the past. Keeping one's feet in the present, sometimes storm-tossed life, requires some basic understanding of where we have come from, but also of where we are going. We will in future chapters have to address how it is that a person can live in the midst of distress with patience.

The Problem of the Missing Context

The truths of Romans 8 are best learned when we are not suffering; but they can only be comprehended when we do suffer. We need to have a rational structure for our lives, and a worldview that can explain both the good and the bad that happen in it. But when a person is shattered and shocked by recent tragedy, it may not be possible to put together the pieces.

One reason why some people are stuck on the question of "why" is because they have not developed a comprehensive view of life. They do not see their lives in the context of a larger whole—that they are part of a whole cosmos, and a certain kind of age in which corruptibility is one of the laws.

Take, for instance, people who ask: "why did God give me this cancer?" or "why did God let my spouse be unfaithful to me?" or "why did God take my job away from me?" The problem with such questions is that the context is missing. Monism is the view that every event of my life has as its immediate cause the direct intervention of God. It doesn't matter that I am part of a whole cosmos affected by sin, fallenness, and corruptibility. For that matter, when it comes to good things happening, monism assumes that God just arbitrarily decided to give some kind of treat. Such assumptions lead to confusion in prayer, and confusion about the apparent lack of evenhandedness in the distribution of blessings in this life.

Consider the following diagram:

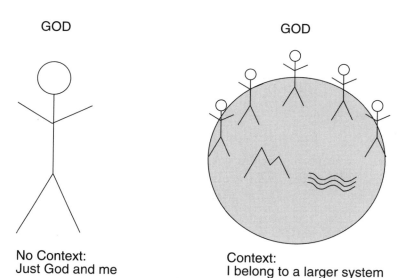

No Context:
Just God and me

Context:
I belong to a larger system

Our experiences are part of a larger whole. Our losses occur not necessarily because God is punishing us for particular sins on our part (although the Bible does say that evil behavior sometimes results in a particular judgment of God; cf. 2 Kings 5:20–27; Acts 5; 12:19b–23; 1 Cor. 11:29–30). Trauma and loss may come as a surprise to us, but the fact that they do occur should not be a surprise.

In other words, we may be shocked by the significant losses that occur, but in the long haul it is not necessary for us to be confused by them. Viewing our lives in their larger context before suffering occurs is the best preventative measure that can be taken to protect us from total spiritual confusion when suffering comes. Here is where pastoral teaching can undergird pastoral counseling.

The Healing of Grief and Trauma

The Scriptures say that it is good to be in the house of mourning, but also promise that mourning will come to an end.

> The lowly he sets on high, and those who mourn are lifted to safety (Job 5:11).

> Your sun will never set again, and your moon will wane no more; the Lord will be your everlasting light, and your days of sorrow will end (Isa. 60:20).

> You will grieve, but your grief will turn to joy (John 16:6).

> Blessed are those who mourn, for they will be comforted (Matt. 5:4).

In the face of loss, even in the face of what feels like total loss, something still remains. "And now these three remain: faith, hope and love" (1 Cor. 13:13). Grief and trauma are healed by those things that remain in the midst of grief and trauma.

Grief and Faith

Grief can be a kind of spiritual crisis, a testing of faith. Anger is a common response to loss, anger sometimes directed at God. The "frustration" that Paul speaks of in the creation, when translated into our experience, is not many steps away from anger. The sense of indignation any person may have about things not being the way they should be will often seek a target. Who's to blame? Who is responsible? On whose door do you knock impatiently?

Was it my fault for not urging my wife to see the doctor sooner? Was it her fault, because she refused to take the radiation therapy that might have saved her life? Was it the doctor's fault for not detecting the lump earlier? Was it the government's fault for not being willing to pay for more advanced testing equipment? Is it really God's fault because he could have prevented her tissues from going wrong in the first place?

Whether or not one can find earthly causes for an episode of suffering, the question often floats up to the ultimate. The philosopher's distinctions of material cause, formal cause, efficient cause, and final cause is played out in ordinary experience as "what kind of a God would allow this to happen?"

Today many people don't bat an eye at expressing anger at God; others view it as blatant blasphemy. Between these extremes is a more honest, saner, and biblical approach. Let us summarize it in four propositions: a) it is not a good thing to be angry at God and can be one of the least constructive positions for us to be in; b) it is naive to pretend believers never get angry at God; c) if someone is angry at God, it is better to admit it than to hide it somewhere it can embitter him or her; and d) there are ways for us to direct our frustration and anger in more constructive ways.

For some reason God saw fit to include in his revealed word expressions of frustration and anger directed at him by some of his most faithful followers. Consider the following passages:

Lam. 2:5: The Lord is like an enemy; he has swallowed up Israel. He has swallowed up all her palaces and destroyed her strongholds. He has multiplied mourning and lamentation for the Daughter of Judah.

Lam. 3:32: Though he brings grief, he will show compassion, so great is his unfailing love. [33]For he does not willingly bring affliction or grief to the children of men.

Jer. 45:3: You said, "Woe to me! The LORD has added sorrow to my pain; I am worn out with groaning and find no rest."

Ps. 43:2: You are God my stronghold. Why have you rejected me? Why must I go about mourning, oppressed by the enemy?

Ps. 42:9: I say to God my Rock, "Why have you forgotten me? Why must I go about mourning, oppressed by the enemy?"

Ps. 22:1: My God, my God, why have you forsaken me? Why are you so far from saving me, so far from the words of my groaning?

Job 14:18: But as a mountain erodes and crumbles and as a rock is moved from its place, [19]as water wears away stones and torrents wash away the soil, so you destroy man's hope.

These are strong words. So too were the words of Martin Luther, writing in his mature years of what was really in his heart as a young monk:

> I did not love, nay, rather I hated, this righteous God who punished sinners, and if not with tacit blasphemy, certainly with huge murmurings I was angry with God, saying: "as though it really were not enough that miserable sinners should be eternally damned with original sin and have all kinds of calamities laid upon them by the law of the Ten Commandments, God must go and add sorrow upon sorrow and even through the gospel itself bring his justice and wrath to bear!" I raged in this way with a wildly aroused and disturbed conscience (Pauck, 1961).

Sometimes people are angry with God because they have nothing or no one else to attach their anger to. Sometimes it's because the loss seems so severe, so wicked, that it takes on ultimate dimensions. Rape, earthquake, murder, war—they all seem to transcend ordinary earthly cause and effect and take on cosmic, spiritual dimensions. Surely here is where evil meets good, so why doesn't good prevail?

Then again, it can happen in those who have a simplistic view of God's relationship with the believer—if I belong to God, he will bless me, and he will never stop blessing me. Again, the problem is the missing context. The person believes that the loss can only mean God has dropped his part of some bargain, rather than seeing his loss as part of the cycle of a fallen creation.

Where we find such experiences in the Scriptures, we don't find God scolding or punishing the angry person. Like all emotions, anger rises and falls. When the time is right there is usually a teachable moment when the person can construct a better understanding.

When a grieving person expresses frustration or even anger at God, a crisis of faith has occurred, but not the abandonment of faith. After all, if someone gives up on faith, he or she isn't going to be interested in talking to or about God at all. More often than not, after the person has vented his or her feelings of anger, there is still a longing to know God and to sense his presence. This was the case with many of the biblical authors who thrashed about with God only to come down to the point of expressing ultimate faith in him. The flow of many of the Psalms follows this pattern: I am oppressed; why don't you help me, God?; yet will I praise him. Faith remains.

Grief and Love

The truth that has more healing and restoration in it than any other is that God does not abandon those he loves. Loss is separation, but it is precisely then that a grieving person needs to know that there is nothing that can separate us from the love of God. The same New Testament passage that gives the sobering perspective of a cosmos that groans and will groan till the restoration also gives this profound word of comfort.

> Who shall separate us from the love of Christ? Shall trouble or hardship or persecution or famine or nakedness or danger or sword? As it is written: "For your sake we face death all day long; we are considered as sheep to be slaughtered." No, in all these things we are more than conquerors through him who loved us. For I am convinced that neither death nor life, neither angels nor demons, neither the present nor the future, nor any powers, neither height nor depth, nor anything else in all creation, will be able to separate us from the love of God that is in Christ Jesus our Lord (Rom. 8:35–39).

Grief follows loss, and another word for loss is separation—the separation of one person from another, of one's spiritual life from an ailing body, of things that seem like they should work together in life: work, security, trust. If the stinging pain of loss is separation, then the greatest comfort is found in the ongoing connection that is to be found in God himself. No separation. That is the believer's comfort. Time and again in the Old Testament God offers the grieving person not primarily answers and explanations, but himself. God offered himself to Job in his afflictions, to Joseph when he was mistreated, to David when he was persecuted, to Isaiah when Israel was threatened; the list could go on.

The pastoral counselor might wonder: Is that all I can offer? After all, this grieving person is asking that the problem be fixed, the loss recompensed. He is looking to me with the pain of separation on his face, how can I simply tell him that God loves him and is with him and that that will be enough?

There are several faults in these assumptions. First, the pastoral counselor will not be able to "fix" the problem of the loss. Distraction is not the answer, replacing what or who was lost is not the answer, assuring the counselee that at some future time the loss will be filled in is not the answer. Second, one does not "simply" tell someone of God's love and presence. They are profound realities, often communicated as much by actions of love and presence in the pastoral counselor than by a simple spoken slogan. Third, the fact of the love and presence of God does not mean healing will come instantaneously. God's processes of healing almost always take time. When it comes to grief and trauma, the effects of pastoral counseling of any sort cannot be evaluated in the short term.

Yet it still is amazing the difference that the love and presence of God (modeled in the love and presence of the pastoral counselor and others) can make. Even without the comprehension of "why?" even when the loss is still recent history, many people find real comfort and a real ability to cope because they have a basic grasp of "I will never leave you nor forsake you."

Grief and Hope

Christian hope prevents grief from being limitless and destructive. "We do not want you to be ignorant about those who fall asleep, or to grieve like the rest of men, who have no hope" (1 Thess. 4:13). To those who have no hope, death is always irreparable loss. Without God, all of life's routine losses accumulate to the point where the person becomes cynical, embittered, and negative about the prospects that anyone has in life.

Hope—in conjunction with faith and love—is able to interpret life's losses as part of the inevitable cycle of downturns and upturns in this life. Hope says that the end of the story hasn't come yet, and because our stories are written by a God who is good, there will be a happy ending.

Consider the exuberant hope of Jeremiah:

> They will come and shout for joy on the heights of Zion; they will rejoice in the bounty of the LORD—the grain, the new wine and the oil, the young of the flocks and herds. They will be like a well-watered garden, and they will sorrow no more. Then maidens will dance and be glad, young men and old as well. I will turn their mourning into gladness; I will give them comfort and joy instead of sorrow (Jer. 31:12–13).

The ultimate hope is eschatological. It is very common for those who believe in heaven to still, somehow, be afraid or even repelled by the thought of it. From what they have been told it seems like total loss. Take away friends, the food we like to eat, the beautiful vistas of the earth, its colors and sensations; replace it all with bleached robes, clouds, and a stringed instrument that is not always a favorite, and it's no wonder there is little enthusiasm for heaven. C. S. Lewis once said that he felt sheepish about not desiring heaven more, but then he realized there is nothing else he had ever longed for. Heaven is the fulfillment of all that is good in this life. If we have depicted it as the negation of what we have known in this life, that is our misinterpretation. The final hope is gain, not loss.

> Now the dwelling of God is with men, and he will live with them. They will be his people, and God himself will be with them and be their God. He will wipe every tear from their eyes. There will be no more death or mourning or crying or pain, for the old order of things has passed away. He who was seated on the throne said, "I am making everything new!" (Rev. 21:3–5).

And even during life in this fallen world, Christian hope offers a better existence. True, the believing Christian admits to great evil and chronic sin-sickness in this life because of the nature of a fallen world, but also sees the ongoing providential acts of God bringing grace, beauty, and love into the world. The Christian prays, as Jesus instructed, "lead us not into temptation, but deliver us from evil";

the Christian believes that there is an ongoing protective work of God, even though we may often not be aware of it.

The Perils of Christian Stoicism

Christians have sometimes sought a quicker and simpler approach to "solving" the "problem" of grief. In it the Christian tries to keep a stiff upper lip, to not cringe at pain, to consider every loss a gain. It is to try to get past tears by not letting them come in the first place, to walk briskly past the house of mourning. Its adherents call it faith, and they are proud that they are untouchable as far as life's pains are concerned.

But even the apostle Paul grieved over many losses in his life; and Jesus' heart was torn by the insult of the death of Lazarus, and at the prospect of his own impending death at Gethsemane.

Such an approach is better labeled pagan Stoicism than Christian faith. The ancient Stoics had a simple view of life and life's fortunes: we are all part of a large impersonal plan, pain is part of the logic or reason of the cosmos, and so the best response in the face of pain is to be unfazed by it. Weakness is found in the person who cares too much about the ups and downs of life.

Stoicism is basically humanistic and anthropocentric. It offers a form of salvation that is self-generated and that produces self-righteousness. It is works-salvation at its worse. On the surface, it appears to be a strong stand taken in faithfulness to God. But since when has the Christian gospel said that faith and neediness move in opposite directions? Was it not the Apostle Paul who said that his tribulations brought out his weakness, and that at the point of weakness and need, his faith was proven?

When Christians believe that the only response faith can have to loss is to be unfazed and uncaring, that the last thing to do is to go whimpering to other people or to God, they put themselves in a position that cannot be sustained and that contradicts every picture of loss, trauma, and grief we find in the Scriptures. No, it is better to go into the house of mourning; to learn what must be learned there, and come out stronger for it.

3

Grief—Coming
to Terms with Loss

Part of every misery, is, so to speak, the misery's shadow or reflection: the fact that you don't merely suffer but have to keep on thinking about the fact that you suffer. I not only live each endless day in grief, but live each day thinking about living each day in grief.

Sorrow, however, turns out to be not a state but a process. It needs not a map but a history.

—C. S. Lewis, *A Grief Observed*

Steve and Sara sat in their pastor's office, stunned, not knowing what to say, ask, or even how they felt. In spite of sitting next to each other, they felt so alone, so distant. Last week they had buried their seventeen-year-old daughter and now nothing made sense, nothing seemed real. Sara spoke of feeling empty and disoriented; Steve said very little. Both had many questions they were afraid to ask. How could she have died? Was she driving too fast? Looking at each other, they silently asked themselves, "What could I have done?" "Why?"

Later that day the pastor met with John who had just received his final severance pay. He had known the plant was closing and had been sending out resumes for months. Now he was unemployed, feeling lost and alone. He could not find words to describe the heaviness and tightness he felt in his throat and chest. Hope seemed so far away.

Before leaving his office the pastor received a phone call from a dear friend who told him her husband had just been diagnosed with cancer. The prognosis was not optimistic and she asked for prayer and a visit. Driving home that evening, the pastor sensed his own heaviness and a vague sense of "How long, O Lord?" The losses of a child, job, friend—life itself seemed overwhelming.

The Nature of Grief

Grief is the natural, expected reaction to a loss. At times grief may seem to loom all around while at other times we may sense we are protected from grief's impact. However, our human condition is characterized by losses; grief weaves itself throughout our life experiences. None of us can escape the grasp of grief.

Grief is our reaction to loss. We are created in such a way that when we experience loss we respond in a manner that facilitates our adaptation to the loss. The purpose of grief is to adjust to the loss and to accept present reality. Grief functions to help us cope in a fallen and sinful world characterized by loss. Complex reactions involving every part of our being constitute the grief experience. This necessary process of adjustment occurs across time and weaves a unique path for each individual.

The experience of loss places one in a state of bereavement. The words *bereave* and *rob* are derived from the same root, which has the connotation of being unwillingly deprived by force or by having something stolen. The loss is unwanted and uncontrollable. The outward display of grief is what we call mourning. One who is grieving is called a mourner. Expression of the pain, confusion, and other reactions are greatly influenced by one's cultural and social influences. The staid, reserved responses of many northern Europeans, and the wailing and crying out characteristic of Middle Eastern cultures are both expressions of mourning, attempts to adjust to loss.

The most significant loss is the loss of life. The Christian has the confidence that to be absent from the body is to be present with the

Lord (2 Cor. 5:8). The deceased person is fine. Those who have not died, the survivors, are the ones confronted with difficult and painful changes. As death is the most significant loss, most examples in this book are drawn from that most common grief experience. Grief responses are similar for any loss and thus examples of coping with a death are relevant for coping with any significant loss. Other examples of losses that may evoke a grief response include:

- a child moving away to college
- a miscarriage
- infertility
- parents retiring in another region of the country
- job transfer
- diagnosis of chronic illness
- financial loss
- a friend's relocation
- retirement
- infidelity by marriage partner
- acceptance of uncaring or rejecting family member
- loss of hope, innocence, time, opportunity, or independence.

Before pastoral counselors can effectively address the needs of those in grief it is important that they understand the complexities of the grief experience.

The Experience of Grief

A woman who had just observed the one-year anniversary of her husband's death stated, "I didn't know I could hurt so much for so long." Grief is a painful experience that involves our entire being, our whole person. Many people think of grief as simply an emotion. While many emotional reactions are involved in the grief experience, grief is much more complex.

Emotions

We have been created with emotional reactions in order to be equipped to modify our understandings and behaviors in an ever-changing world. Emotions assist us in identifying what is changing, modulate our energy so that we may make changes, and help us reorganize our beliefs and expectations so that we can accept the changes. Table 3.1 defines our basic emotional reactions (other emotions, such as frustration, can be understood as a combination

Table 3.1
Emotions and Their Functions

Emotion	Purpose, Information Provided
joy, happiness	continue, this is good
acceptance	affiliation, safety
anticipation	this is new, explore
surprise	unexpected, stop and get oriented, be alert
disgust	reject, this is "poison," push away
anger	something is wrong or I have been wronged; change something in my situation or within myself to correct the wrong
sadness	a loss has occurred; adjust to the loss, adapt to being without what was lost; accept; let go of control
fear	danger is present; I must change the situation, learn to cope within the situation, or escape/avoid the situation; fight, flight, or cope
hurt	I have been harmed or abused; discontinue or avoid
shame	I want to hide; I feel disconnected from someone; I want to reconnect

of these emotions) and the information that they provide us about what is changing.

Grief is a complex assortment of many reactions, not merely emotional reactions. Yet many strong emotional reactions occur when we mourn. The surprise of the loss may immobilize, stun, even paralyze a person. Nothing may be felt (often described as feeling numb). The news of the death of a loved one may initially shatter one's psychological well-being and sense of safety. The news doesn't seem real. Everything seems to stop, nothing else is important as the news begins to sink in.

Once the news of the loss begins to seem real, deep sadness often overwhelms a grieving person. Much like a tidal wave that engulfs a small island, sadness overwhelms every aspect of experience. Sadness is our emotional reaction to the perception of a loss. When sad, we experience little or no energy and feel a heaviness, weight, or a stabbing pain. The feelings of sadness may be so great that the mourner may attempt to escape from them. However, taking care of others, keeping busy, using alcohol, or acting like everything is "okay" can only temporarily mask the sadness. The body and soul cry out while adjusting to the loss.

Sadness is resolved through acceptance of the loss and the readjustments in life necessitated by the loss. The necessary readjustments may be seen clearly in the case of the death of a spouse after many years of marriage. When Martha died, William sensed that his entire world became disorganized. Retired for many years, they had shared routines with each other, and, without being aware, had developed intricate habitual patterns of relating and functioning. These patterns addressed all of life's activities, including their social and relational lives, their emotional well-being, and many practical activities. With Martha's death came huge holes in William's expectations, habits, and routines. When he wanted to ask a question or share a thought he found there was no one there. William noticed, two months following the funeral, that he no longer had coffee with his morning paper—Martha had always made the coffee. This realization brought on a deep sadness with an outburst of tears. Having slowed down, he realized that he needed to face the loss of his mate's activity (making coffee), and he chose to make the coffee himself. From that day on, William returned to having coffee with his morning paper. He had successfully readjusted to this small detail in his life, a life changed by his loss. A mourner is continually confronted with such little details that require readjustment. Mourning may be understood as the process of experiencing each life detail that had involved the loss, feeling the emotional reaction to the loss, and making the adjustments required to continue living in spite of the loss.

Acknowledging the loss and making the necessary adjustments may elicit anger. Mourners often feel anger but are unaware of the object of their anger. A mourner may be angry at the loss or the cause of the loss. Something inside cries out, "this isn't right!" and "I don't want it to be this way!" The function of anger is to identify that something is wrong and something needs to change. A loss signals something is wrong and the emotion of anger results. Consider, for instance, the imprecatory Psalms (e.g., Ps. 109) in which loss and injustice prompt indignation in the writer, an anger that in one sense drives home the reality of the loss.

The object of the anger is often confusing to the mourner. Can I be angry at an impersonal corporation who, through a reorganization, eliminated my job? Can I be angry at someone who has died? Can I be angry at a rapid growth of cells they call cancer? Can I be angry at God? I know I'm mad at something, someone!

When we are angry, our whole being may cry out for something to change. We want back what was lost. The thoughts may be, "if only . . . then I'd be okay." But what we want most, having what has been lost, is not available. We don't want to adjust to the loss. The anger may be manifested in irritation toward others, overt anger or rage expression, withdrawal from God, or even a kind of withdrawal from the self, such as perfectionistic demands or even self-contempt.

Since we cannot change reality, i.e., reclaim the loss, we are confronted with needing to change ourselves, which is part of the adjustment to the loss. Changing ourselves will involve acceptance of the loss. Ultimately, it is acceptance that will resolve the anger. Often the energy, focus, and determination of the anger are absolutely necessary in order to make the changes loss demands. Many changes often must occur before a person can embrace acceptance.

Being unable to reacquire what was lost may first lead to anger and then to despair. "I can't keep going on" are words often spoken by people in deep mourning. Incidents of suicidal thoughts are greater following a significant loss. Hope seems far away. To regain a sense of control, some develop resentment. Despair feels like being out of control, whereas anger and resentment increase our energy and sense of personal control. Resentment requires an object, something to resent. The object may be what was lost, the fact that I can't have what was lost, those who still have what I lost, or God.

The cost of despair and resentment are high. Not only do these emotional reactions greatly tax our physical bodies, they also contribute to social isolation, difficulties in relationships, unrealistic thinking, and avoidance of reality. A time of passage through despair is often necessary to accept the loss. However, we are not designed to live in despair or bitterness. The pain of the grief experience can motivate us toward resolution.

Fears, both rational and irrational, often increase in both frequency and intensity. Initially, fears may involve "how will I make it without . . . ?" or "what is going to happen next?" Many losses involve circumstances that clearly produce dangerous situations. For example, when a young father dies, who will now help with the parenting and financial support? If I lose my job, how will I support myself and my family?

Other fears, possibly less tangible but equally real in experience, are also cued by a loss. When a loved one dies from cancer it is common to fear that you will develop cancer as well. Every pain or physical abnormality may now seem threatening. After experiencing the pain of a loved one's death, many fear loving again. Without being consciously aware, they distance themselves from others. The loss of employment or an opportunity may create fear manifested by a loss of confidence or hope. Will I ever get a job again? Am I finished in this area? Fear of going crazy or never being able to be happy or safe again are not uncommon.

Fear can prompt either paralysis or action. On many occasions, one's anger facilitates the energy and definition to adjust to the changes and thus decrease the fear. William's fear of going out alone after Martha's death diminished as he felt angry at the thought of missing his granddaughter's graduation. He had always relied on Martha's people skills in public situations and now feared not knowing what to do or how to act. How would others treat him now? Yet he was angry that he wanted to avoid such an important event. His anger energized and motivated him to move out of his isolation and toward relating to others.

For many, the loneliness of loss produces the greatest pain. When the loss is death, the longing for connection with the deceased and resulting loneliness cannot be directly soothed. Direct contact with the deceased will not again occur in this life. The loneliness may generalize to a sense of being different or isolated from others. No other person has had my experience, my relationship with the deceased, or knows what I am feeling now.

Other losses, such as moving to a new community, unemployment, a natural disaster, or even losses attributable to normal events such as the youngest child's first day in school or saying goodbye to a child as he or she leaves for summer camp, may also trigger loneliness. Again, the experience of the loss is unique to each individual and our uniqueness is highlighted by recognizing the change, the absence of what used to be.

Another emotional reaction to the loss in connection between people is shame. This painful emotion prompts us to hide, cover over, and protect the self. Thoughts concerning guilt commonly occur when we feel shame. This emotional reaction prompts us to look for a cause, to ask "what have I done?" that caused my pain or "what could I have done?" to have avoided this loss. The emotion of shame is the pain that many experience which prompts them to withdraw, hide, blame themselves, make excuses, or avoid. Before the sin in the garden, Adam and Eve had no shame. But with their transgression came a rupture in their relationship with God, and with it, an overwhelming need to hide.

Why do we feel shame following a loss? Does this mean we have done something wrong, or not done enough? No, it is because we perceive that we are disconnected from others, ourselves, God, or some object or value. Shame functions to bring our attention to the disconnection and is resolved with reconnection. Many of our losses, such as losses through death or losing someone's approval, can never be reversed; we cannot have reconnection with the specific individual. The reconnection that will resolve the shame feelings, this deep pain, will be found somewhere else. New connections with other people, God, the self, and even objects and values need to develop.

The resolution of grief reveals acceptance. Both an emotional reaction and a willful decision, acceptance involves a sense of peace and safety. With acceptance comes a sense of predictability, adjustment to the loss, and a return to a sense of personal control in one's life. Trust returns, albeit in a less naive, more mature form than before. A sense of joy and happiness may return as a result of acceptance. With further adjustments, the memories of what has been lost can be integrated into the present experiences. William, proudly enjoying his granddaughter's graduation, can appreciate how Martha had been a good grandmother and how she contributed much to who his granddaughter was becoming.

The cost of ignoring our grief emotional reactions can be enormous. Physical illness, broken relationships, social withdrawal, spiritual starvation, and significant psychological impairment can occur. Our emotional reactions are given to us by our creator to help us adjust to changes in our world, as is evident in the Scriptures where they portray every possible emotional experience: fear, affection, anger, sorrow, etc. The emotions that accompany grief prompt us, even drive us, toward making the changes of acceptance and readjustment.

Physical Responses

Grief involves a reaction of the total self. Many report feeling "sick" upon hearing of a significant loss. Immediate physical responses can include a sense of exhaustion, lack of physical strength, paralysis, trembling, shaking, twitching, heart palpitations, tachycardia, and nausea, diarrhea, or other gastrointestinal distress. Shortness of breath or rapid, shallow breathing may occur, as may a sense of being smothered or choked. Swallowing may be difficult and some report feeling as if something is stuck in their throats. Headaches or other body pains may be experienced. The body may be tense with involuntary muscle spasms in some situations. Chest pains, hot flashes or chills, excessive sweating, and a dry mouth may also be experienced. When confronted with the loss, a person may feel dizzy or faint. The initial physical reaction often involves a significant disruption of all physical functioning.

Some experience symptoms of anxiety upon hearing the news of a significant loss, or being reminded again of the loss. Shortness of breath, smothering sensations, dizziness, chest pain, an exaggerated startle response, and hypervigilance may occur. Sleep may be disturbed, as may concentration. Emotional outbursts, often involving either anger or fear, may "appear out of nowhere." In addition to the pain of the loss, these symptoms feel very distressing.

These reactions are often short-lived, ranging in duration from moments to hours. However, some experience these symptoms for days or longer. An episodic return of these reactions is common. After feeling well for days or weeks a person may have a bout with nausea, a headache, an episode of trembling, or some other physical reaction. Such recurrence of these symptoms may be associated with an anniversary of the loss, with a conscious awareness of some aspect of the loss, or for no apparent reason.

Any of these physical grief reactions can persist over time. In addition, hair loss and diffuse or vague physical complaints may occur during mourning. Such complaints often involve a diffuse chronic pain and may involve gastrointestinal, cardiopulmonary, neurological, and gynecological systems. The physical symptoms may remain long after the individual is consciously aware of grieving or may return long after the loss.

Thoughts/Beliefs

Grief tends to impair one's concentration, orientation, memory, and general thinking processes. Making decisions and solving problems may become difficult, seemingly impossible at times. As the emotional reactions of sadness and shame become intense, they interfere with thinking processes. Mourners may describe themselves as if in a daze, disoriented, or confused. Even details like time, date, and their present location may be difficult following an awareness of the loss.

The initial reaction to a significant loss is disbelief. It is as if one's psychological system is not yet prepared to incorporate and use the information. Many of our mourning rituals, such as the viewing of the body following a death are intended to address this reaction of disbelief. Research has shown that those who are not able to view the body of a deceased loved one display greater difficulties in resolving their grief.

A preoccupation with the loss accompanied by ruminations or obsessions is common during the first days, weeks, or months. Thoughts of the deceased may seem ever present; reminders are everywhere. The expectations of the deceased being involved in the day-to-day activities often continues long after the funeral. A car pulling into the driveway, the phone ringing, or the cat knocking something over may cue an expectation that the loved one is home once again.

Self-esteem tends to decrease as mourners become more sensitive to their inadequacies and perceived deficits. Their desire to reclaim what was lost, to reconnect with what is now not available, focuses their attention on their own limitations and inadequacies. Their thinking is likely to become pessimistic. Motivation diminishes in the confusion. Life may now seem to have less purpose, value, or direction. Disillusionment may set in. Questions with no answers can hound the mourner. The "why?" question takes many forms yet rarely does an answer feel satisfying. In the initial phases of grief the longing is for the return of what has been lost. "Why?" is more of a plea and expression of pain and confusion than an intellectual query.

The mourner is confronted with a deep need to make sense of the loss. If someone or something can be blamed, if only some good could come from this, then maybe acceptance can follow. Mourners may wonder if they are guilty in some way, which may make more sense of the problem or give more of a feeling of personal control. In many ways, survivors take responsibility for what has happened, for not preventing the death, for surviving and not dying. No matter how illogical, they feel responsible.

Identity is altered with such a loss. The survivor can no longer say "we" or "us," but now "I" or "me." The unemployed person is no longer an employee or wage earner, no longer can use titles or identities previously held. At a deeper level, the definition of self is now altered as mortality is confronted, the loss and potential for further losses accepted.

The why questions, the awareness of the loss and resulting pain, the confusion all have a spiritual impact. For some the loss draws them closer to God, recognizing that only God can offer comfort and safety at such a time. Others sense God has abandoned them. The psalmist cries out "How long, O LORD? Will you forget me forever? How long will you hide your face from me?" (Ps. 13:1). The mourner applies to God the sense of disconnection and the pain of the separation.

For many, the grief experience involves vacillation between being drawn closer to God and times of anger, feelings of abandonment, and confusion. The adjustments to the loss bring changes in how one views one's own life and how one views God. The world may seem less safe, less attractive, less friendly. Many turn to God only when no other answer is available, when all other avenues have proven futile. As the adjustment continues, changes in priorities, values, expectations, and hopes become evident. Material objects often are less satisfying; relationships are given more value. Psalm 13 concludes with a resolution: "But I trust in your unfailing love; my heart rejoices in your salvation. I will sing to the LORD, for he has been good to me" (Ps. 13:6–7).

Perceptions

Our perceptions, the mental processes by which we recognize and interpret our experiences, are also impacted by grief. They form the building blocks for our emotional reactions and thoughts. Following the death of a loved one, it is not uncommon for survivors to report sensing they heard the deceased speak, saw them in another room, or to have a sense of the deceased present with them. Mourners are often comforted by these perceptions, although they may be reluctant to tell others about them, fearing others will not understand or think they are going crazy. For some mourners such perceptions cause fear. Reassurance of the normalcy of such experiences often relieves the fear and brings comfort.

Feelings of unreality, dissociation, depersonalization, or sensing a loss of self may occur in those who are actively mourning. The awareness of the loss may so disorganize mourners that they become confused at the most basic levels regarding their own sense of self, their own identity. This may last for hours, days, or longer. Individuals who were dependent or defined themselves through their relationship with who or what was lost are most at risk for this type of reaction.

Defenses and Attempts at Coping

Our psychological being automatically attempts to adjust to the awareness of a loss. Coping strategies or defenses are activated so that we can function in the present and begin the readjustment process. For many, the first reaction is denial, an insistence that "this can't be true." The denial may range from momentary disbelief to viewing the body and believing the person is still alive. Denial can take the form of shock, numbness, and a sense of unreality. The news of the loss may be too great to accept, integrate, and act on initially. These defensive (protective) strategies allow one's psychological system to prepare to adjust to the loss.

Others experience repression (an automatic response) or make a conscious choice to avoid or suppress thoughts, emotions, or memories of the deceased or other loss. Memories of being with the deceased may not be available or the mourner may avoid looking at pictures of the deceased, going into his or her bedroom, or talking with anyone about the deceased. Yet others experience an opposite reaction in which they actively search for the deceased, even though they have a conscious awareness of the death. For some, this becomes a symbolic search for meaning—a desire to find a purpose in life or meaning in the death.

An identification with the deceased is evident in some situations as a survivor may focus on being similar (with the goal of being identical) to the loved one. The survivor may take on attributes, characteristics, mannerisms, or interests of the deceased. In doing so, the identity of the survivor may be masked, the emotional reactions of sadness, pain, anger, and shame suppressed.

Regression to an earlier stage of life and coping is also evident in some situations. For some, strong dependency traits and childlike behaviors become evident, while others display the independent and self-indulgent behaviors common to adolescence. Acting out may be a means for expressing some anger yet is ineffective in adjusting to the loss.

In a similar manner some attempt to take care of others as a means of coping in their own situation. During the funeral or other events following the loss mourners may find responsibilities thrust upon them. They may focus on others, thereby gaining a perception of being in control and a normalizing of the experience. However, if this pattern becomes excessive, they may block themselves from making the adjustments they need to make in order to reorganize their lives.

These defensive strategies and coping styles may be effective in the short term as survivors begin their adjustment to loss and all the implications of loss. As the defensive strategies begin to interfere with their ability to cope, as the coping styles are more of a liability than an asset, the individual is motivated to adjust to reality. This process of change is functional and healthy. Problems develop when the coping style becomes rigid and people maintain a defensive strategy, even though the strategy interferes with their ability to cope with daily realities.

Behaviors

Grief disrupts all life functions, even the most basic like sleep and appetite. Many have problems falling asleep or having sleep unexpectedly interrupted. Some fear sleep, worrying about the dreams that they may have. Others find sleep an escape from the painful awareness of the loss and sleep excessively. Rising in the morning may mean having to continue the painful adjustment process. Many lose interest in eating and may eat only out of some vague sense of needing to eat. For others, eating may provide comfort or soothing. In such situations, mourners may overeat in an attempt to buffer the pain.

Some experience searching behaviors: scanning or looking for the deceased. The sounds coming from another room may be interpreted as the presence of the deceased, shopping in the mall may include looking at a crowd "just in case."

Many behaviors become disorganized and mourners often experience being absentminded and poorly organized. Effectiveness and efficiency often decrease. Lacking a sense of meaning, mourners may engage in meaningless or repetitive behaviors.

Avoidance of activities that had involved the deceased is common in the early phases of grief following a death. Mourners may avoid events that have symbolic value; for example, a family avoiding the normal dining room after the death of family member, eating in front of the TV on trays instead. Dinner becomes a time of relative isolation, the TV doing a numbing work while the dining room is quiet and empty.

The probability of self-destructive behaviors, such as risk-taking or alcohol or substance abuse increases following a significant loss. Mourners tend to be more accident prone. Many display impulsive or acting out behaviors, possibly as a means of expressing or blunting their pain.

Over time changes in lifestyle occur. Behavior patterns from before the loss now must be reorganized. New behavior patterns emerge: how time is spent, the chores that are done, relationships with others and with God. It is not uncommon, for instance, for a mourner to have difficulty going to church or attending a regular fellowship function. The person may feel under scrutiny or may simply feel too emotionally fragile: for instance, in the case of a spouse who no longer can sit in church with his or her deceased partner. A spiritual event can feel like open-heart surgery; everything inside gets exposed. During the adjustment of the mourning process, the person is likely to return to prior patterns.

Social Relationships

A significant loss, of any type, impacts one's ability to be vulnerable, open, or available to relate to others. The threats to self-esteem encountered in grief further impair social relationships. Initially many mourners experience one of two extremes: they lose interest in others as they focus on the loss or they greatly desire not to be alone and want others around them. For some this is manifested in increased dependency, clinging behaviors, and an expressed fear of being alone. In both situations, the relationships are changed as the mourner now is focused on his or her own experience and may have little or no empathy for others. This is a normal initial reaction as the psychological system is overwhelmed by the loss.

If the loss involved either a significant person or a significant life event (such as a job, church, or a move to another locality), all social behaviors are likely to be disjointed. The habits, expectations, and patterns of relating are no longer the same. William, who's wife had died months ago, still avoided church; he had never sat alone. There didn't seem to be a place for him as he saw couples everywhere. Steve, a middle-aged man who lost his job, sensed he did not belong anywhere. Feeling alienated from others, he did not know what to do with himself, with his time, or who to be with. Old friends were working or had now relocated; he felt shame when with employed men since all he had ever known was his work. Following a significant loss many feel like there is no longer a place for them.

Jealousy of those who still have their spouse, their job, or who seem not to have had a loss may occur. For many, this jealousy is accompanied by anger, why questions, and shame. "How can I be jealous? I can't wish this pain on anyone. I can't believe I'm thinking this way"—all common thoughts (some fleeting, others fixated) of mourners. These reactions illustrate how every aspect of one's being is challenged by the demands of adjusting to the loss.

A basic need of all people is to have connection with others. Loss is a disconnection, resulting in the emotion of shame that then inhibits the person from meeting their need to connect. The social needs of a mourner include being with others, sensing that others are still available, that others still care, that the mourner is not disconnected from everyone. Mourners need to know that others can listen to them, can hear and understand what they are sharing. With repetition, the social connections pave the way for the acceptance of what has been lost and the reality of what remains.

Grief Myths

Grief is a pervasive reaction to the perception of loss that requires a multitude of changes. In understanding the nature of grief, it may be helpful to consider common myths about it.

Myth #1. *All mourners need to do to resolve their grief is to get their feelings out.* Grief is much more than an emotional catharsis. The task of grief is to adjust in all affected areas of life.

Myth #2. *Grief is resolved when the mourner can put the loss out of his or her mind.* In truth, signs of grief resolution involve being able to think of the deceased or what was lost realistically and with a variety of emotions.

Myth #3. *Mourning is usually over in three months and certainly within one year.* Various biblical passages have been used artificially to support a time limit on grief (e.g., 1 Peter 1:6). But grief continues until the mourner has made the necessary adjustments to cope well in light of the loss. For example, a mourner may initially focus on the problems of the moment that need attention, such as insurance transactions. This rational, decision-making activity may help a person move through the first couple of weeks. However, if the person continues in this mode, he or she may not express and resolve his or her emotional reactions, which could lead to depression, bitterness, or withdrawal. For some mourners and some kinds of losses this is a brief time, while for others the rest of their lives will be influenced by the loss.

Myth #4. *Grief is resolved in a linear fashion, i.e., the intensity is great initially and tapers off over time.* The pattern of grief is unique to each individual. A grief reaction may be elicited many years after a loss if the readjustments required have not yet occurred. For example, a widow who has happily remarried and enjoys her new life may many years later experience a return of her grief reactions when she hears an obscure song that she used to sing when she was dating her deceased husband. Her grief reaction does not mean that she has not successfully grieved her loss nor does it mean she is not loving her second husband. Rather, the stimulus of the song has cued memories and emotions that must now be rearranged.

Myth #5. *One can judge the degree of love someone had for the deceased by the intensity and length of his or her mourning.* It is not uncommon for a mourner to subscribe to this belief. By doing so, the mourning does not serve its purpose but rather results in a continuation of the pain and blocks the readjustment. At times, focusing on an intense expression of mourning is self-serving as the mourner can obsess about the loss and not engage in the changes readjustment requires.

Myth #6. *Each loss is grieved separately.* Our capacity to adjust to any given loss is in part dependent upon what other losses, and thus adjustments, we are currently experiencing. Losses can be cumulative and, given that we have finite coping abilities, a seemingly small loss can cue an intense grief response.

Myth #7. *Death before age 100 is premature and unfair.* Our affluent, technological age has contributed to our unrealistic expectation of a long, healthy, pain-free life. We are only a couple of generations removed from what most of the world still experiences— a life expectancy of 40 years or less.

Myth #8. *Life is fair.* God has promised not to abandon us, to be with us, and to indwell us. We have also been told that life in this sinful world does not operate on a simple set of "fair" rules. Jesus' life certainly demonstrated the unfairness in human experience.

By being realistic in our understanding of grief we can grieve more effectively and help those who are grieving. In addition, a realistic acceptance of the nature of our world and our existence can facilitate a resiliency and strengthen our faith so that when we encounter loss we are better equipped to cope and to adjust.

The Process and Purpose of Grief

Grief is experienced across time and for the purpose of adjusting to the loss. A painful experience, grief is a process in which changes occur so that the mourner can function in reality. Grief resolution is evident when the mourner no longer anticipates or is impaired by the loss. When the book of Ecclesiastes says: "there is a time for everything, and a season for every activity under heaven. . . . A time to weep and a time to laugh, a time to mourn and a time to dance," and that "it is better to go to a house of mourning than to go to a house of feasting," and "the heart of the wise is in the house of mourning" (3:1, 4; 7:2, 4) it is speaking not only of the inevitability of grieving, but also its *purposefulness.*

Losses take many forms. Most often we think of *physical loss,* such as a person's death or the loss of a possession. Physical losses are tangible, often acknowledged by others.

A second type of loss, *psychosocial loss,* also elicits grief. Psychosocial losses involve things that are intangible, relational, symbolic, or spiritual, psychological, or social in nature. These intangible losses have special meaning to the person experiencing them that may or may not be recognized by others. The effects of these symbolic losses are unique to each person.

What do people grieve when lost? They grieve anything that is of value to them. Physical losses include loved ones, one's body (e.g., in the case of amputation), possessions, pets, and other things. Psychosocial losses can include lost opportunities, a broken engagement, divorce, unemployment, loss of freedom, hope, dreams, energy, purpose, youth, security, friendship, independence, or any other valued aspect of life.

Most physical losses and some psychosocial losses are *primary losses*, i.e., those that are clearly recognized by the mourner and others. Primary losses are the initial focus of the grief. The death of a loved one is very often a primary loss and those who are mourning are often (at least initially) comforted by others. *Secondary losses* occur as a result of primary losses and are often not recognized by others. For instance, the death of a spouse, which is a primary loss, results in many secondary losses. The widow or widower experiences the loss of a social and economic partner, companion, lover, confidant, coparent, and friend. Daily habits and rituals are disturbed; life is disorganized. In a similar manner, the loss of a job will produce the primary loss of income and may elicit secondary losses of opportunities, hope, friendships, and even one's identity.

It is often the secondary losses that are the primary focus of the mourner. These losses are the most personal and often have the greatest impact in day-to-day life. It is also these losses that are least likely to be recognized by others. Mourners can find comfort and connection by recognizing their secondary losses.

Grief Theories

Grief is a universal human experience and has received much attention from psychological researchers and theorists. Two theories, those of Elisabeth Kubler-Ross and Theresa Rando, have provided useful insight into our reactions to loss and the process by which humans adjust. The first theory identifies stages through which a mourner passes in the grief process while the second set of theories identifies tasks or processes that must be accomplished to resolve grief.

Kübler-Ross Stage Theory

Working with terminally ill patients, Kübler-Ross organized her observations of the grief process into her stage theory of grieving. Kübler-Ross hypothesized that we proceed through five stages following loss or anticipation of loss (Table 3.2).

Table 3.2
Kübler-Ross's Stage Theory of Grief

- Denial
- Bargaining
- Anger
- Depression
- Acceptance

Upon acknowledging loss or anticipated loss, the person experiences shock and disbelief. Initially, the acknowledgment is only cognitive and only later does one allow one's emotional reactions to be experienced. This first stage is the beginning of the readjustment process and leads to a full realization of the loss. The person hopes the loss will not actually occur, or has not actually occurred, or hopes that it will not be permanent.

Bargaining, the second stage, may involve dialogue with God in an attempt to undo the loss. Promises may be offered or deals proposed in the form of "if only you will undo the loss." Such bargaining does not change the reality of the loss.

Confronted with the futility of bargaining, the mourner becomes angry: anger at the loss, anger at God, anger at not being able to have the loss undone. If there is any possibility the death could have been prevented it is likely that anger will be directed toward individuals or institutions. Hospitals, doctors, police, or others who may have been involved in the circumstances surrounding the death may be targets. This anger increases the sense of control experienced by the mourner but continues to protect the person from full acceptance of the loss.

The fourth stage, depression, occurs after anger has run its course. Now the loss and its implications cannot be denied, ignored, or changed. Sadness and other emotional pain may consume the individual as he or she is confronted with the reality. (The distinction between grief and clinical depression will be further addressed at the end of this chapter.)

Ultimately, sadness and other emotional reactions assist the individual in adjusting to the loss. A new cognitive and emotional organization develops and the person can experience peace. Acceptance, the final stage, marks the resolution of the grief.

This stage theory has been widely used in understanding the grief reaction. However, a mourner or pastoral counselor needs to be cautious to recognize that these stages are descriptive of a process that may not be a linear, sequential series of events. For example, many who grieve do not engage in bargaining. Furthermore, a mourner who is angry may return to bargaining or alternate between anger and depression.

Task Theories

Task theories focus on what needs to be done to resolve grief, i.e., the work or processes of grief. Grief involves a great deal of work or effort, as changes and adjustments are difficult. A pastoral counselor may observe a mourner involved in these tasks, understand the purpose of the mourner's present coping behaviors, or may choose to facilitate movement in a task. These models can be helpful to the counselor, serving as a general map of the work of grief.

The tasks are a sequence of life events that must occur for successful readjustment to the loss. The mourner will move through the tasks, engaging in the work for the specific task. Each aspect of the loss will require the mourner to move through the sequence of tasks toward adjustment. Mourners move through these processes at different rates for different aspects of the loss. For example, a widow will proceed through these tasks for the primary loss of the physical life of her husband. In addition, she will process these tasks for each of her secondary losses (the spouse as companion, coparent, confidant). Within each of these there are many subcategories that will involve processing through the tasks. The tasks are moved through sequentially for each issue. A widow may be on a different task (i.e., different levels of adjustment) for each of several issues at the same time.

We will review two such models. Warden's model (Table 3.3), a simple description, recognizes the denial stage outlined by Kubler-Ross and identifies the need for both intellectual and emotional acceptance. Following these different types of acceptance, the mourner is confronted with continuing in life, a life now void of the deceased. Finally, living is enhanced, and grief resolved, through the withdrawal of attachment and emotional energy from the deceased (or whatever was lost) and reinvestment in new relationships. It is not that the mourner no longer cares about the

Table 3.3
Task Theory of Warden

1. Accept the reality of the loss.
2. Experience the pain of grief.
3. Adjust to the new reality in which the deceased (or whatever was lost) no longer exists.
4. Withdraw emotional energy from the relationship and reinvest in new relationships.

deceased, but rather the mourner has been freed to accept what was in the past and to live in the present. The deceased is never replaced, but rather the mourner is freed to build new and different relationships.

Rando's model (Table 3.4) incorporates the work of Warden and expands on the delineation of grief work. She identifies six processes categorized into three phases. The first phase, *avoidance*, involves recognizing the loss and overcoming the shock and denial. The denial, a buffer necessary for many to begin the adjust-

Table 3.4
Task Theory of Rando

Avoidance Phase
1. Recognize the loss.

Confrontation Phase
2. React to the separation.
3. Recollect and reexperience the deceased and the relationship.
4. Relinquish the old attachments to the deceased and the old assumptive world.

Accommodation Phase
5. Readjust to move adaptively into the new world without forgetting the old.
6. Reinvest.

ment process, may be accompanied by outbursts of anger, sorrow, or fear. For others, the news may result in their caring for others. This can be helpful to the individual and those around them, yet at some point each person must recognize the loss.

The *confrontation* phase makes the loss real in the mourner's experience. Reacting to the separation will necessitate the experience of one's emotional reactions to the loss and the secondary losses. The third task, recollecting and reexperiencing the deceased and the relationship, facilitates the mental and emotional reorganization that is necessary. Mourners have a legitimate need to tell their stories, to recall and reflect. At times, the mourner will frame the lost relationship in unrealistically positive terms, denying the problems that had been a part of the relationship. In such a situation, the mourner may be on the third task for the reality of the loss of the person but on the first task for the reality of the relationship. As mourners move through the first three tasks they reach a point where their need to talk about the loss decreases. At this point they begin the fourth task, relinquishing old attachments.

Letting go of what has been lost (both the primary and secondary losses and all of the expectations, hopes, and dreams invested in them) prepares the person to more effectively live in the present reality. The *accommodation phase* leads to a new relationship with what or who was lost and the freedom to invest in the present.

How long does this process take? The answer to this question is complex. Recall that the mourner will move through these tasks for each aspect of the loss. Thus, the pastoral counselor may understand a mourner to have resolved the grief regarding many aspects of a loss and still be deeply involved with other aspects.

Is mourning worth all the work and pain? While the experience at times may suggest not, the alternative to grieving is not to adjust to present reality. Failure to grieve a loss or an aspect of a loss leaves that person still attached, invested in what has been lost, and impaired in relating to others, to God, or to himself or herself in the present.

Grief and Specific Populations

In the course of pastoral care, grief situations of many types arise. While the tasks of grief appear to be universal, the issues and methods of grieving vary greatly. It is difficult to predict the response of any specific person from group data. Yet increased awareness of the tendencies, learned patterns, and salient issues can sensitize pastoral counselors and increase the probability that they will connect in a meaningful way with mourners.

Grief and the Death of a Child

Nothing seems as unjust as the death of a child. The cause of death does not seem to matter. Rather, the loss of one who seems to have so much potential, so many life experiences ahead, seems so unfair. While less common than in generations past, over 50,000 children die each year in the United States. Our cultural expectations of a long, healthy life leave us unprepared to cope.

Families are forever changed following the death of a child. It has been shown, for instance, that grief over the death of a child is often stronger in the second year than the first.

Parents desire never to forget their child, but this healthy desire can inhibit the grief process. Such parents may think that if they adjust, if they live well now, that they will forget and it will seem like that lost child is no longer important.

Family members need to talk about the deceased child, to recount stories and share their emotions. In doing so, they will be reassured that they will not forget the child and that others who are close to the family will not forget the child as well.

One's own death is often contemplated, even to the point of wishing for or considering suicide as a way to be with the child. In one study, 50 percent of mothers of deceased children no longer looked for happiness but were waiting for their own death.

A search for meaning, a cause, or a reason for the death is common. Approximately 70 percent of parents who have had a child die seek spiritual solutions and increase their commitments in religious communities. Many seek to be reunited with their children in heaven yet also are looking for meaning in a painful world. A significant and lasting change in values occurs in which traditional Western values of achievement and success are diminished and the values of family, relationships, and spirituality are strengthened.

While most family members make a positive adjustment to the loss, a phenomena called *shadow grief* often remains. This lingering grief is always in the background and behind everything else and may persist throughout life. Anniversary dates, such as the date of the death, Christmas or other family holidays, when the child's class graduates, or when the child's friends marry may elicit further grief responses. This normal reaction requires further adjustments, further letting go so that the mourner may invest in the present world.

The death of children not yet born also elicits grief. A miscarriage, even in the first few weeks, is very likely to elicit mourning. Frequently the woman will initially blame herself, or, to a lesser degree, her husband. Grieving this loss is complicated if others did not know about the pregnancy. No one will have had the same attachment to the developing child as the mother. She will likely experience fantasy about what the child would have been like, how he or she would have looked and acted. Her husband is likely to focus on action or diversion, wanting to get on with life. In addition, if any attention is received by the couple during their mourning, it is likely to be directed toward the wife, further alienating the man from his grief. In recent years, much has been learned about the mourning following an abortion. Similar to the grief response following a miscarriage, postabortion grief is complicated by the willful decision to have an abortion and often by a time delay between the loss and the recognition of the loss.

The death of a child frequently elicits conflict between the couple. Couples who have experienced the death of a child have a higher incidence of marital separation and divorce. Often, each spouse expects the other to grieve in the same manner he or she does and senses the other is denying pain. A recognition of the very different experiences and relationship with the developing child can facilitate understanding and diminish conflict.

Many Christians mourning the death of a child have found a measure of comfort in the words of King David who, after his newborn son died, came to the realization: "Can I bring him back again? I will go to him, but he will not return to me" (2 Sam. 12:23). David had grieved terribly while the child was sick, but, after the death, was comforted in his grief by the promise of eternal life for his child. The parent suffers the pain of separation, but comes to know that the child is secure in the care of God. One young woman whose child was stillborn and who went through the full intensity of grief knew early in the process—indeed, just two days after the death of Alex—that the love of God would be her refuge. She wrote to her child:

> N'er my breast shall give you suck
> Open your eyes and take a look
> You stayed peaceful as you were
> Undisturbed and safe.
>
> You looked so beautiful in my eyes
> But rest assured, God is wise
> I shall not worry where ye shall be
> You're in God's love eternally.

In the long term, her grief was worked out through the help of a support group through a local hospital, and she ended up having a ministry to others going through the same tragic circumstances.

Grief and Men

Learning how to be a man in Western culture involves many lessons that complicate the grief process. Traditional masculine values, such as being strong and taking charge, interfere with the work of grief. Letting go and accepting the loss seem incongruent with masculine traits.

Men tend to grieve alone, in silence. Little is said. Men tend to return to work or another activity soon after the loss and busy themselves with activities. During the initial stages of grief, men are often in the role of making decisions, caring for others, making sure everything is taken care of. Grieving may seem as if it is left for the women and children. Following the funeral or the initial adjustment to the loss, men often find the focus is now less on grief and more on "moving on." Having barely begun their mourning, they bury themselves in work or increase their use of alcohol or other substances. A widower is likely to visit the grave alone and express his pain through crying, words, and other expressions—but in solitude. Others in his life may have no awareness of his graveside visits or tears.

Feeling out of control, men are more likely to take legal or physical action in response to a significant loss. For some, grief is replaced by anger, aggression, and even violence. Risk-taking behaviors may increase as a demonstration of perceived personal power and life. The use of alcohol, drugs, or other substances may increase.

While the pattern of solitary, silent mourning is common, it is important to note that this pattern may be out of perceived necessity rather than choice. In addition to sex role learning, men often receive messages from others that cue them to keep their pain private. A question such as, "how are the kids holding up?" directs the focus of the man's grief toward others. Men frequently want to express their thoughts and feelings, and when given a chance in a safe situation tend to express themselves. A recent study of widowers found that 97 percent of the men expressed relief when given a chance to express, to be heard.

How can men be given a chance to be heard? Men often need some time to determine if it really is safe to proceed, and an acknowledgment of the appropriateness of expression. Direct questions such as, "How are you doing?" "Are you sleeping okay?" or statements such as, "I've been concerned about you" may help establish the initial connection. Furthermore, men tend to benefit from multiple contacts, returning days later and continuing with the contact. A follow-up call, a breakfast, a basketball game followed by some quiet time can facilitate a continuation of the expression and sharing necessary for grief resolution.

Grief and Children

Children who experience great loss, such as the death of a parent or sibling, have the same grief work, the same need to adjust to the loss, as adults. However, children must make these adjustments within the parameters and limitations of their developing abilities. Furthermore, as they mature through new levels of thinking, emoting, and relating, they may have to grieve the loss again in the context of these new abilities.

A child's concept of death develops from no awareness of time or permanency during infancy to an adult understanding. Preschool children think of death as a nonpermanent sleep, a reversible event. School-age children (ages 5–9) often think of death as coming from the outside, from a monster, or an angel who takes away life. Even at this age death is thought to be something that can be reversed, outwitted, or avoided. In the child's thinking, "If I do the right things, death will not happen." When death occurs, children are likely to blame themselves, to experience an unrealistic sense of responsibility.

As the children mature and begin to develop abstraction abilities, they understand death in biological terms and as irreversible, though distant and avoidable. It is common for teenagers to alternate between fears of death and risk-taking behaviors, with a sense of being invincible.

A child's mourning is greatly influenced by the developmental stage. Fears are common, often fear of further loss, such as the surviving parent dying, or fear of going to sleep. Often, children experience a loss in safety and security and regress to earlier coping strategies. School-age children may return to sucking their thumbs or carrying a blanket following a parent's death. Children long to know they will still be protected, cared for, and not alone.

Anger toward the one who died, toward the loss, or toward the survivors caught in their own grief is also a common reaction. They may experience abandonment and conclude they are unimportant, weak, or powerless. In the immature thinking of a child, it may seem that the parent died because the child was bad or not loved by the parent. Many children have interpreted the death of a loved one as a punishment. Others have thought their anger "wished" them dead or that somehow they made the death occur.

The understanding of children, limited by their stage of development, is often confused. Not only do they have difficulty understanding what are the implications of the death, they are also confronted with unexpected changes in all areas of life. How does God fit into this? Even young children take some comfort in thinking

"Mommy is in heaven," yet may be angry or feel left out that they can't be there also. Children long to be reconnected with the deceased. Their need to be connected in a relationship must be a primary focus of their caregivers.

Children who experience a significant loss at a young age will need to adjust to the loss at each subsequent developmental stage. Initially, children make adjustments to loss with the coping and cognitive resources available to them. As they develop and acquire more sophisticated ways of understanding, their immature understandings are inadequate to account for their experiences and the consequences of their loss. At each developmental stage children and then young adults will grieve their loss with their current coping abilities.

Adults need to be sensitive to the child's stage of development and need to allow, even facilitate, the child's expression of their thoughts and feelings. One young woman shared that as a child she was told "God loved your mommy so much he took her home to heaven to be with him." It is not surprising that this young woman had difficulty seeing God as good or loving. How could a loving God be so selfish as to rob a child who needs her mother so he can enjoy her company?

Children, like adults, need to proceed through the tasks of grief. How they proceed is greatly influenced by their level of development and how the adults in their world are mourning.

Grief and Cultural/Racial Differences

Mourning is a learned ability acquired in childhood through observing family members and others react to death and other losses. Different cultures develop their own strategies for processing grief. In northeastern Brazil, for instance, where there is a very high infant mortality rate, mothers express very little grief upon death. Other groups express a great outpouring of emotion, such as Egyptian mothers, who may display wailing and crying for days or weeks followed by years of muted depression, the suffering serving as a link to the deceased. Still others manifest their grief through somatization (physical symptoms that mimic illness, such as the chest pain of "a broken heart"), aggression, or psychologization. Western cultures have tended to define grief in terms of the symptoms and problems of the experience rather than appreciating the value and purpose of grief.

Pastoral counselors need to be sensitive to the cultural and racial background of mourners in order to understand their grief process. It may be helpful to ask them about grieving in their past, about how others in their life mourned. Listen for their description of the task they are presently involved in rather than assuming they should be doing something specific or expressing grief in a particular manner. Pastoral counselors bring their cultural training and expectations with them and need to be aware of their own reactions.

Complicated Grief

The normal tasks of grieving are difficult, painful, and tremendously challenging. For some, the work of grief becomes overwhelming and problems in living occur like depression, anxiety, and somatic disorders (physical problems with psychological causes). Grief may be complicated by the nature of the relationship at the time of the loss. For instance, the unexpected accidental death of a spouse shortly after a major argument may elicit shame in the survivor, inhibiting him or her from adjusting and increasing the likelihood the survivor will blame himself or herself for the death. Grief becomes complicated when the tasks of grief are not accomplished, when the acceptance of and adaptation to the loss are not achieved. Rando, who has written extensively on complicated grief, noted that mourners with complicated grief "(a) deny, repress, or avoid aspects of the loss, its pain, and the full realization of its implications for the mourner and (b) hold on to and avoid relinquishing the lost loved one" (1993, p. 149).

Complicated grieving interferes with grief work. Depression, anxiety, or other symptoms that develop interfere with daily living. To resume the grief process, the symptoms must be alleviated as the symptoms prevent the mourner from facing the loss, the pain, and the required changes. These symptoms can function as defenses, distractions, or barriers to acceptance and healing. Complicated mourning may take many forms. Four of the most frequently seen by pastoral counselors are *depression, chronic mourning, anxiety,* and *somatization.*

Depression

The emotional reactions of grief and depression have many similarities. Furthermore, many of the behavioral and social responses of healthy mourning are similar to depressive symptoms. In both, sadness, despair, confusion, and decreased motivation are evident, as are social withdrawal, and decreased activity and interest in usual life opportunities. Physical pain and other somatic complaints may occur in either grief or depression. With so many similarities, how can the pastoral counselor discriminate between healthy grief and disabling depression?

One salient difference is the focus of the mourner's experience. Healthy grief focuses on the loss while depression tends to be more diffuse, less well-defined. The purpose of grief is apparent in healthy mourning while depression tends to seem to be without purpose. The pain may be described as useless or cruel by the depressed mourner; whereas the nondepressed mourner understands the pain as an acknowledgment and consequence of the loss.

A second significant difference involves relating to others. Depressed individuals tend to experience social withdrawal and resist others, seemingly pushing away others' actions of caring, concern, or support, while nondepressed mourners tend to receive such signs of caring. When given an opportunity to talk, to be heard, mourners often begin to share their stories and feelings while depressed mourners show little interest in speaking. The nondepressed mourner finds comfort in being connected, whereas the depressed mourner is not affected or even becomes irritable and agitated.

The role of anger may also be an indicator of the presence of depression. During mourning, anger tends to be directed at something involved in the loss. The anger may be directed toward the cause of the loss, an illness, the deceased, God, or even the self. It has a defined target. The target may switch, but is still connected with the loss. In depression, anger is less well defined, less focused on a target. Often the anger becomes directed against the self in a vague yet pervasive way, as if the person has turned against himself or herself. In grief, anger serves the purpose of defining what is wrong and what needs to change, while in depression anger is often disguised, unfocused, directed against the self, and seemingly not leading to any change.

These differences are patterns of behavior rather than single episodes. Healthy grief at times involves diffuse anger or the sense of loss of purpose. When these patterns are consistent and stable then depression has set in. Jacobs and Lieberman (1987), after reviewing the research, offered the following five criteria for diagnosing depression in mourning:

1. the depressive pattern has lasted longer than six months;

2. it occurs later rather than immediately after the initial news of the loss;

3. it includes pervasive disturbances of self-esteem, psychomotor retardation, or suicidal gestures;

4. it causes severe subjective distress or impairment in social or occupational functioning;

5. the individual has a personal or family history of depression.

Physical symptoms that persist for several weeks, such as weight loss, loss of appetite, or sleep disturbances, may also indicate that a depression is developing. These physical consequences will further inhibit the mourner's capacity to do grief work.

A depressive reaction within a grief episode necessitates the treatment of the depression and the resolution of the depressive symptoms before significant grief work can take place and the acceptance and readjustments occur.

Chronic Mourning

The natural course of mourning is toward resolution. At times, some display an intense acute grief reaction that does not appear to significantly change over the course of time. The nature and intensity of their symptoms appear unchanged from the early days of the loss. Chronic mourning may alienate others or become a means by which the mourner gathers attention or support. This pattern may provide a symbolic connection with the deceased. Mourners may fear that if their mourning diminishes they will lose the last connection or that it will seem like they no longer care.

Mourning may be manifested in many ways. Grief expression becomes dysfunctional when adaptation to the loss does not occur. This may range from a refusal to acknowledge the loss to not releasing what has been lost. If reinvestment in the present is not possible, the mourner is engaged in a dysfunctional pattern.

Pastoral responses to chronic mourning need to be broadly based. An understanding of the functional role the mourning plays is necessary to plan how to intervene and assist in the grief process. Trust, validation of the reality of their pain, and safety/security issues will all be factors in ministering to the mourner. Often, the severity of the situation may necessitate a referral to a counselor who specializes in grief counseling.

Anxiety

Anxiety symptoms are frequently not identified during the grief process and, if left unchecked, may pave the way for depression. Anxiety may be manifested by episodic panic attacks in which the individual senses a loss of control, great distress, impending doom, and significant physical arousal (e.g., increased heart rate, breathing rate, and excessive muscle tension). Phobic responses (the fear or avoidance of an object, person, or place) are also common. The phobic object may be dinner with the family, a room in the house, or social contact. Mourners may also display generalized anxiety, a state of hyperarousal, or ruminations and obsessions.

These anxiety symptoms become detrimental when they impair the individual from adjusting to the loss and investing in the present. Anxious symptoms are common in the grief process; however, if they persist and block the grief work, they must be addressed. Treatment may include skill training for the management of anxiety and, in some situations, medical interventions (antianxiety medications).

Somatic Symptoms

Somatoform disorders are physical symptoms that mimic biological or medical disorders but for which there are not demonstrable organic causes or apparent links to psychological processes. Grief reactions often involve brief somatic symptoms, but can be prolonged and thus interfere with grief work. The symptoms may mimic those leading up to the death of the loved one or may be disabling. In such cases, people attribute their difficulties in coping with life and maintaining normal responsibilities to their physical problems, often denying or minimizing the impact the loss has had. Such individuals tend to be very resistant to change, are well-defended against interpretations of their symptoms, yet, when given an opportunity, may be able to share their hurt, fears, anger, and pain. Helping resolve these somatic concerns is often a long and complex process.

No matter what form it takes, complicated grief is a pattern often resistant to change. Pastoral counselors will likely see such situations frequently as most mourners move through the grief process within the context of their support networks and personal coping skills. When these are insufficient the pastoral counselor is often called upon to assist in the process.

Grief, the natural, expected reaction to a loss, is a *purposeful* process. We are designed to grieve so that we can adjust to what has been lost. This adjustment process involves who we are as uniquely created beings in combination with the skills and resources we have acquired in our personal histories and our present-day social supports. And here is where Christian counselors have something more to offer. "We do not grieve like the rest of men," were the words of the Apostle Paul. We do grieve, but in our grief we have available the hope for restoration (not replacement) beyond our losses. Loss in some ways can even be turned into gain (Phil. 3:8), only because there is an infinite God who stands as Lord over all reality.

Most often we are able to cope and adjust to losses and reinvest in the present. However, there are circumstances that occur that place such demands on our capacity to adjust that our systems are overwhelmed. These are traumatic events.

4

Trauma—Overwhelming Our Capacity to Cope

I will take refuge in the shadow of your wings until the disaster has passed.

—Psalm 59:1

Steve was jarred awake by the ringing of the phone. He looked at the clock—it was only 4 A.M. Picking up the receiver, he slowly said, "Hello?" A serious, seemingly distant voice told him his wife, a nurse who worked nights, had been in a very serious auto accident and that he should come to the hospital. Suddenly, Steve was alert, focused on solving the problem of child care while he was at the hospital. He drove calmly to the hospital, not feeling, not worrying, and was even aware that he was very calm. Upon his arrival, he spoke with the doctors and was told his wife, Sherry, would be fine but needed surgery.

Sherry did not lose consciousness in the accident. As the cars collided, she saw and heard the impact in both slow motion and real time. She felt the pain of her broken and bleeding body but sensed she didn't care nor was she worried. She expressed concern for the other driver and asked the paramedic to let her husband and children know she was all right.

Two years later Sherry still has difficulty driving after dark. Her heart races and her whole body tightens each time she hears metal hitting metal. Sometimes Sherry is wakened by nightmares in which she sees herself in the car just before and during impact. Steve experiences a moment of panic each time the phone rings when Sherry is not home.

Ed served his country with distinction and has been successfully employed in the same job for almost fifteen years. Some of his coworkers and friends have noticed an occasional twitch or frozen look on his face. Sometimes he experiences flashbacks of his combat experience twenty years ago. For just a moment, he can see the fire in the village, smell the burning, and hear the screams. Fear, anger, and shame sweep over him. While these flashbacks often only last a couple of seconds, sometimes they have lasted many hours. Ed constantly fears another flashback is about to occur. He now lives alone, socializes infrequently, and is often the last one to arrive and the first to leave a church service.

Betsy also experiences flashbacks but her pain does not involve other people in faraway lands. When Betsy closes her eyes, she sees "him" leaning over her, about to touch her. On so many nights of her childhood, Betsy pretended to sleep while "he," her father, came into her room and molested her. Now a mother of two young children, Betsy experiences great anxiety, fear, and shame when she thinks of her husband touching her and has had several panic attacks while attempting to be sexually intimate with him. She feels very alone, helpless, and afraid.

The Meaning of Trauma

Each of these people have experienced trauma. As was discussed in chapter one, trauma may be defined as *the experience of something shocking happening to someone (physically or psychologically) that produces some kind of inner injury and affects the person's ability to function in normal ways.* Trauma is a combination of the *events* that happen and the *effects* on people and their *ability to cope* with the events. Something is traumatic when horrible events overwhelm a person's ability to cope with these events, resulting in psychological, spiritual, and physical wounds. A person who has been traumatized has experienced a shock that interferes with his or her psychological, physical, emotional, spiritual, and social well-being and development. The effects of a single traumatic experience may last a lifetime. The Scriptures portray both the reality of trauma in the world (famine, flood, murder, rape, war, accidents, etc.) and how God helps people who are the victims of trauma.

Trauma overwhelms our ability to symbolically represent reality in our minds, to be able to make sense of what is happening, and to link our present experience with who we are. Many theorists and researchers have used the concept of *schemata*, which are the basic building blocks of our minds, our symbolic representations of reality. A schema may be defined as an organizational unit of the mind, a knowledge structure, which is stored in memory and consists of elements of past experiences and reactions. Schemata develop out of our learned experiences and allow us to organize and operate in the world. For instance, a child growing up in a safe, secure home will have a schema of reality in which the world is safe, whereas a traumatized child may have a schema in which all of life is dangerous and insecure.

The works of Piaget on cognitive development are useful in identifying how schemata are impacted by trauma. Piaget theorized that three processes are constantly in effect as any person attempts to make sense out of and live in the world. These automatic mental processes strive for a balance between bringing new information into our existing understandings and changing our understandings in light of new situations. *Adaptation*, the goal of development and our thinking in general, is a process by which our internal symbolic schemata become functionally similar to external reality. When this occurs we are able to predict what will happen and derive meaning and connection in our experience. Adaptation is achieved through the tension between two other mental processes. *Accommodation*, a process that modifies existing schemata to fit new information, allows one to learn new things by stretching, expanding our present understandings. The corresponding process, *assimilation*, allows for the present schemata, or cognitive structures, to identify and function in the present situation. New information is incorporated into existing schemata and a person can interpret a new situation in light of previously obtained knowledge. Adaptation occurs when assimilation, which allows one to understand the world in the context of one's existing knowledge, is balanced with the integration of novel information in such a way that one's symbolic representations are similar to objective reality.

Our capacity to symbolically represent reality within our minds allows self-awareness, consciousness, and identity. Our relationships with each other and God are dependent upon our ability to maintain realistic schemata. Most situations in life can be adjusted to by a combination of organizing them into already existing understandings (assimilation) or by modifying our definitions, expectations, and representations of them (accommodation). For example, a young child may have a schema that suggests that all adults are good. When this child encounters a new adult, assimilation results in the child experiencing the adult as good. As the child ages there are disappointments with some adults and the child experiences great internal tension as the original schema cannot adequately represent this. Accommodation occurs when the child's schema changes to: adults are good but sometimes disappointing. Adaptation is achieved as the child's symbolic representations reflect reality.

Now assume this same child is subjected to an experience in which an adult family member becomes very violent. This traumatic event overwhelms the child's schemata, which are unable to account for this deviation from expectations. The child is unable to make sense out of the experience, cannot determine how to attribute responsibility for the violence, and has a hard time having confidence about predicting what will next occur. The assumptive world has been shattered and the child may experience fear, anger, shame, anxiety, and withdrawal. Long-term modifications to the schemata may take many forms. If unable to achieve adaptation such children's schemata may now be primarily characterized by either accommodation or assimilation. As young adults these individuals may view the perpetrator as essentially all good, denying or minimizing the violence that occurred. They may assimilate this violent trauma into their existing schemata of good adults. This may lead to overdependence, choosing spouses who are abusive, or a tendency to blame themselves when others wrong them. When they experience anything that reminds them of the violence, they may sense being overwhelmed but not be aware of the cause. Or, another possible reaction may be to view all people (or all women, men, adults, etc.) as potentially violent and dangerous. Such individuals may have a pessimistic, sarcastic, or paranoid view of life. The schemata are modified so that the danger possible in life is accounted for but not the other aspects of life.

Both of these coping responses only account for an aspect of objective reality. Such schemata may offer an illusion of being protected and in control but will lead to decreased vulnerability and flexibility in adjusting to changing life circumstances. Adaptation, the modification of the schemata through the processes of assimilation and accommodation, allows people to account for the good in a situation (or person) as well as the danger, the need to be vulnerable and to have protection.

A person who is exposed to trauma experiences a pervasive sense of powerlessness. Many traumas involve a physical powerlessness, the literal experience of being physically overpowered. Even more threatening and distressing is emotional and mental powerlessness, the inability to make sense of what is happening and the lack of a sense of personal control and well-being. One's entire existence is disrupted, nothing makes sense, the self is overwhelmed. It is as if the traumatized person has no category and no mechanism by which to organize or make sense of the experience. This pervasive sense of powerlessness is extremely distressing as the traumatized individual may experience multiple forms of pain that may seem beyond his or her capacity to cope.

Historical Understandings of Trauma

It is widely recognized that some people who have been exposed to trauma are greatly and negatively impacted. Following the Civil War, the U.S. Government established residential homes for soldiers who were unable to reintegrate into society (the precursor to our Veterans' Administration programs). The German physician Eulenburg in 1878 referred to the effects of trauma as "psychic trauma," which he noted involved crying out, fear, and extreme shock. He attributed this condition to a concussion of the spine. In an attempt to account for the same behavior patterns, a contemporary, Oppenheim, described "traumatic neurosis," which he theorized resulted from molecular changes caused by electrical processes in the central nervous system.

A second understanding of the cause of these symptoms was proposed in the late 1800s. Sigmund Freud and others (Charcot, Janet, etc.) suggested that the sense of powerlessness and other symptoms following trauma were not due to a physical cause, but rather, to psychological processes. They theorized that the memories of traumatic events are split off, dissociated, denied, or otherwise unavailable to conscious awareness, yet influenced the person's behavior and experience. Freud vacillated between believing the trauma that influenced a person was a veridical, historical event or a fantasy, an unconscious wish of the patient.

The wars of the twentieth century have provided many opportunities for the study of the effects of trauma. Physicians observed that many soldiers during World War I displayed great fear and anxiety, even after apparent danger had ceased. Most explanations involved a physical cause, for instance, "shell shock"—the supposed physical problems resulting from exposure to the concussions produced by exploding shells. This explanation was inadequate as many soldiers who were never exposed to combat developed the same symptoms. For example, many medical personnel well behind the lines who treated the maimed and dying developed similar symptoms.

The devastation of World War I greatly affected many psychological theorists who had an optimistic view of human nature but now were appalled by the human capacity to destroy. Freud further modified his theories to account for the symptoms he observed in those who had been traumatized. He noted that they experienced intense fear, anxiety, helplessness, and a high degree of physical stimulation that they could no longer modulate. Their thoughts and sensations focused on the trauma, even many years later. He noted that humans are limited in their capacity to cope with trauma and, when their capacity is exceeded, they continually relive the traumatic event as if trying to adjust to what has happened.

During World War II much research was done on treating and protecting soldiers from the effects of trauma. Now termed "traumatic neurosis," the focus turned from a physical cause to psychological factors. The term "combat exhaustion" was used to account for the sense of being overwhelmed by the trauma.

One can see the developing understanding of trauma in recent years by how it has been defined in various revisions of the *Diagnostic and Statistical Manual*, used by mental health professionals as the system of diagnosing psychological disorders. In 1952 the *DSM-I* labeled reactions to stress as "Transient Situational; Personality Disorders" under the category of "Gross Stress Reactions." The *DSM-II* of 1968 showed less interest in the effects of trauma and termed reactions to trauma as "Transient Situational Disturbances" and "Adjustment Reaction during Adulthood." Such reactions were thought to occur following overwhelming strains in the environment, such as war, unwanted pregnancy, failure in school, violence, or retirement.

In the past twenty years there has been more extensive research on trauma, and thus only recently have we begun to understand the pervasive effects of trauma. Subsequent revisions of the *DSM* turned to research on stress and reactions to stress to account for the reactions to trauma. The pioneering work of Hans Selye and his description of the General Adaptation Syndrome has provided the conceptual foundation for understanding the impact of traumatic events. Stress was defined as any demand on a person, with some demands being positive (eustress) and others being negative (disstress). Selye observed that the body had a characteristic response to any type of stress. Initially, the body enters an *alarm stage* during which the body is prompted to either fight or flee. Physical arousal increases greatly as the body is prepared to cope with the demand. If the stressor is not quickly resolved or removed, the individual moves to stage two, the *resistance stage*. The body's resting rate is now higher than it had been before the stress, manifested in such ways as increased blood pressure, increased heart rate, or a decrease in the efficiency of the immune system.

Human beings have limitations in their ability to cope. If the stressor is not resolved, the person enters the third stage, *exhaustion*. The body's ability to cope is depleted and the individual may experience fatigue, feeling overwhelmed and anxious, and display fears, depression, or physical illness.

The consequences of being exposed to trauma show up in the effects of stress. The concept of Post-Traumatic Stress Disorder (PTSD), a cluster of symptoms that may occur following exposure to a traumatic stressor, was formally introduced in *DSM-III* (1980) and has been subsequently refined in *DSM-IV* (1994). The symptoms or characteristics of this disorder, highlighted in Table 4.1, include psychological dysfunction, such as emotional fear, anxiety, disturbances in thinking (poor concentration, memory impairment), and sensory disturbances (hallucinations, flashbacks). In addition, significant physical impairment is evident as well, such as hyperarousal (e.g., excessive physical tension and increased heart rate and blood pressure). The effects of being exposed to trauma involves both psychological and physical changes.

The effects of trauma can be great, even debilitating. For some, these characteristic responses to trauma are evident immediately following the traumatic event. Others may appear to cope well during and following the event and display symptoms only after an extended time period. For example, some children who experience sexual abuse manifest disturbances in their functioning immediately while others show no outward effects for a decade or longer. An adult life event, such as having a child the same age as the person was when the abuse occurred, may trigger the stress reactions. Survivors of the Mount St. Helens volcanic eruption and the California earthquakes have displayed this pattern as well. Anniversary dates, the birthday of someone who died in the disaster, or subsequent news coverage have all been identified as triggers for PTSD symptoms.

Intrusive thoughts, feelings, sensations, and perceptions are some of the most distressing symptoms of PTSD. These phenomena often intrude with no warning or cue. These flashbacks, as they are called, can seem very real and elicit the thoughts and feelings that occurred at the time of the trauma. Dreams that symbolically represent the trauma may also seem very real and be accompanied by intense emotions. There is often also a reaction to the flashback itself. A person may feel terror during the flashback and fear and anger about it.

How many people are affected by trauma in such dramatic and disabling ways? Research estimates vary widely depending on the

Table 4.1
Summary of Diagnostic Criteria for
Post-Traumatic Stress Disorder

1. The person has been exposed to (witnessed or personally experienced) a traumatic event that included both an actual or threatened serious injury to self or other, or death, and the person's response involved intense fear, helplessness, or horror.
2. The traumatic event is continually reexperienced in one or more of the following:
   - recurrent and intrusive distressing memories of the event;
   - recurrent dreams of the event;
   - acting or feeling as if the traumatic event were recurring;
   - intense, painful psychological distress when exposed to either internal or external cues that symbolize or were associated with the trauma;
   - and physical reactivity when exposed to cues associated with the trauma.
3. Persistent avoidance of cues or stimuli associated with the trauma and a numbing of general responsiveness (not present before the trauma), as indicated by at least three of the following:
   - efforts to avoid thoughts, feelings, or conversations associated with the trauma;
   - efforts to avoid activities, places, or people associated with the trauma;
   - inability to recall an important aspect of the trauma;
   - significant decreased interest or participation in important activities;
   - feeling of detachment or estrangement from others;
   - restricted range of affect (emotions, e.g., inability to love, express anger);
   - and a sense of foreshortened future (e.g., not anticipating a normal life span).
4. Persistent symptoms of increased physical arousal (not present before the trauma) as indicated by two or more of the following:
   - difficulty initiating or maintaining sleep;
   - irritability or outbursts of anger;
   - difficulty concentrating;
   - hypervigilance;
   - and an exaggerated startle response.
5. These symptoms have a duration greater than one month.
6. These symptoms significantly interfere with the person's ability to function in social, occupational, or other important areas of life.

(paraphrased from *DSM-IV*, 1994)

methods used and populations studied. Lifetime prevalence rates from community-based studies suggest that between 1 percent and 14 percent of the total population will experience PTSD. Those in high risk populations, such as soldiers, people encountering natural disasters, or individuals living in high crime areas, display a far greater incidence of PTSD, with a lifetime prevalence rate ranging from 3 percent to 58 percent (*DSM-IV*, 1994). A church of 500 people is thus likely to have 5 to 70 people who have been greatly impacted by trauma. The experience of a traumatic event can permanently and significantly change how the brain functions and even the size of structures within the brain. The effects of trauma are not limited to psychological consequences but can change one's physical body. Objective neurological and hormonal changes can permanently alter how one may process information or respond to stressors. In high crime areas or places where there have been natural catastrophes the numbers may include half the congregation.

There are many variables that determine how specific individuals will experience a given stressful situation: external events (stressors), the natural consequences experienced (effects), and the coping responses of the people involved (impact). Something becomes traumatic through the interaction of these three variables. What is traumatic for one person may or may not be traumatic for another. A review of these variables may aid the pastoral counselor in being aware of the nature of the stressors encountered and the options in helping those who have been traumatized.

Traumatic Events

What makes an event traumatic? All traumatic events involve a loss or a potential loss but not all losses are traumatic. In a traumatic event a person is rendered helpless and perceives danger. Injury or death have either occurred or appear likely to occur; the event seems overwhelming and dangerous. Traumatic events are not the typical losses that regularly occur in life. Rather, they significantly threaten a person's safety or are of such intensity or magnitude that they would overwhelm most people's ability to cope.

The degree to which an event is stressful (and thus potentially traumatic) is influenced by the following:

- the anticipation or experience of physical or psychological pain;
- the experience of life changes (the more numerous the changes, the greater the stress);
- the cumulative amount of the stressors in one's life;
- social support, such as friends or family (the less the support, the greater the perceived stress);
- potential coping options or resources (the less the options or resources, the greater the perceived stress);
- ambiguity or suddenness of the event;
- and the emotional and mental characteristics and present state of the individual.

Normal losses in life are not considered trauma. The loss of a job, a child marrying and moving to another state, the death of a parent are events that will likely have a great impact on a person. These losses, however difficult to cope with, are typically not traumatic since they are within the scope of common human experience. However, even these events may be traumatic if the person's capacity to cope is seriously compromised—the variable here being the person rather than the event. "Trauma" typically refers to events outside the normal scope of daily living.

The intensity of trauma or the degree of damage an event causes in a person's life is determined by both the characteristics of the event and the individual person's capacity to cope with the event. Some events, such as the death of one's family in a fire or a rape would be traumatic to anyone. Trauma may occur even if a person observes a harmful event. For example, a person who witnesses a brutal killing may be traumatized and display similar reactions as one who had actually experienced direct physical violence.

Natural catastrophes such as floods, violent storms, volcanic eruptions, landslides, avalanches, earthquakes, fires, tornadoes, and hurricanes are often traumatic because we assume our environment is stable and predictable. As traumatic as natural disaster can be, human-made catastrophes appear to have a more negative effect. The negative effects of the trauma are likely to be greater if the disaster was caused by humans, greater yet if the trauma was caused by an intentional act.

To understand how some event becomes traumatic it is necessary to appreciate our need to have meaning in our lives, to make sense out of what is happening. When traumatized, we cry out "Why?" Distressing events caused by natural forces (e.g., flood, earthquake) seem more readily acceptable than a willful malicious act of one human against another.

Wars have provided researchers ample opportunity to study the effects of trauma. Much of the early psychological research regarding trauma focused on veterans traumatized in combat. The harsh, cruel realities of killing are not limited to soldiers. People who live in war zones, the families who find themselves in the middle of a war, are also traumatized by the tremendous losses of life, health, welfare, and safety. The effects may be immediate or may impact following generations.

Violence is not limited to wars. Violent crimes in the United States have risen over 500 percent from 1969 to 1990. During this time the crimes have become more brutal and depersonalized. The reported incidence of rape and other forms of sexual assault against children or adults have risen over 400 percent between 1980 and 1990. Most violence is not perpetrated by strangers but by family members and acquaintances. Various forms of severe child abuse afflict many of our children. Others have been tortured for the pleasure, political causes, or beliefs of others. The human capacity to harm and abuse others, evident from the first human family, perpetuates traumatization.

Another form of trauma is auto and motorcycle accidents that kill as many people annually as the total number of Americans killed in Vietnam. Industrial accidents, diving accidents, and other accidents in transportation (train, airplane, bus, etc.) may also evoke PTSD symptoms.

Vicarious exposure, observing something shocking and overwhelming, may also be a traumatic event. Seeing someone killed or badly injured may in and of itself be traumatic.

In general, the effects of the traumatic event are greater under the following circumstances:

- the trauma is caused by humans;
- there is a significant threat (or perceived threat) to life;

- there is exposure to death, dying, or destruction;
- a person (or persons) of emotional significance are harmed or lost;
- the trauma happens suddenly and unexpectedly;
- it is ongoing;
- it results in displacement or disruption in one's home community;
- there is a potential for recurrence;
- moral conflict is elicited by the events;
- the traumatized person identifies that he or she had a role in the event.

In identifying these factors, it must be remembered that how any given event impacts any specific person is dependent not only on the characteristics of the event but also the characteristics of the person.

Effects of Trauma

Exposure to trauma produces a pervasive and overwhelming sense of powerlessness, an acute disruption of our entire existence, great discomfort, and many changes in physical functioning. Trauma involves loss, the loss of a sense of personal control and well-being as well as multiple other losses. Responses to trauma include the grief reactions in all of their complexity but are not limited to them. The effects of trauma are pervasive, involving every part of our being, and may be long-lasting.

Helplessness

People have an inherent need to perceive some control in their lives, to sense that their behavior influences what happens to them. Trauma overwhelms our capacity to cope. When deprived of this sense of control, when people perceive that they are helpless, they experience great distress and impairment in their abilities to function. Trauma is overpowering. The overwhelming loss and excessive demands to cope exceed their capacities, resulting in the perception of helplessness. In many situations, this perception is veridical; we are temporarily overwhelmed by others or forces much greater than ourselves, such as a raging river or violent criminal. In other situations, the anticipation of harm, the perception of grave danger, impacts a person in the same manner. The perception of helplessness, independent of the cause, has predictable effects.

Research during the last 30 years has shown that the effects of being exposed to uncontrollable events can lead to *learned helplessness*. First studied in animals and then in humans, this phenomenon occurs when people experience events or consequences that are not related to their behavior. How they behaved did not change what was happening to them; their behavior could not change or fix a situation. If a tornado, earthquake, or hurricane is occurring, nothing I do can change the damage done by these forces. What I can do at the moment if I am being robbed, raped, assaulted, or attacked is minimal or nothing at all. In combat, a soldier is helpless to stop incoming shells.

Such situations prompt great emotional distress affecting the ability to think, to solve problems, or even process memory in a typical fashion. Such persons tend to become lethargic, unmotivated, and believe that they are helpless in many areas beyond their traumatic experience. Depressive and anxious symptoms are common.

When they feel helpless, people try to figure out why, often seeking causal explanations. If they believe the cause was outside of themselves, was temporary, and is unlikely to recur, they are less likely to have a sense of helplessness. However, if they conclude the cause of the trauma was due to themselves, was stable or ongoing, or was global and likely to recur, helplessness is probable.

Sometimes people attempt to regain a sense of control, to minimize their sense of helplessness and vulnerability, by blaming themselves. If I blame myself then I have some control over future occurrences and may be able to derive some meaning from the situation. To regain safety, I have to make sure I never do that again. It is common for abused spouses to blame themselves for the violence they have experienced. Survivors of accidents may blame themselves for the death of others.

Our need to have control or influence in our world is a central human characteristic. The pastoral counselor can facilitate the beginning and continuation of recovering from trauma by facilitating situations in which the traumatized person manifests personal control.

Physical Consequences

In the past the study of trauma vacillated between focusing on psychological and physical causes and effects. Our present knowledge base indicates that both perspectives have merit since the entire person is impacted by trauma. Underlying our psychological functioning is our physical body, a body that is constantly seeking *adaptation* in a manner very similar to our psychological processes.

Exposure to even one traumatic event can permanently alter one's neurological and hormonal systems. Animal research has demonstrated that both biochemistry and brain structures may be altered following trauma. Such animals display increased reactivity to even mild stressors, impaired learning and coping abilities, gastric ulcerations, and impaired immune system functioning. In addition, animals exposed to trauma are more likely to self-administer substances of abuse, drugs that may block pain or cause euphoria. These same behavioral changes are observed in people who have been traumatized.

Exposure to trauma during early childhood appears to have significant effects. Children are born with a minimally developed brain; early life experiences impact the maturing brain. Animal research has demonstrated that early trauma decreases the brain's ability to learn from experience. Animals who, while young, experience trauma have difficulty learning to cope, are less dominant, and appear more distressed in later life. Learned helplessness experiments with rats have demonstrated differences in brain structures following exposure to trauma. Some research protocols have demonstrated that a single traumatic event can produce these effects.

What is happening that accounts for these changes? Research in recent years has begun to answer this question. One set of findings has identified the neurophysiology of the increased physical arousal following trauma. The body has several mechanisms that equip it to respond to danger. The noradrenaline system modulates the arousal of the body for emergencies, functioning like the gas pedal in a car. The more fuel given, the faster it goes. Noradrenaline and adrenaline facilitate the fight or flight response, the stress response (GAS) that Selye defined. Heart and respiration rates increase, the muscles under the skin draw tight to prevent excessive wounding (producing "goose bumps"), and blood flow is redistributed with flow decreased in the hands, feet, and internal organs and increased in the skeletal muscles and brain. Pupils dilate, blood coagulates more quickly, and the senses become focused on potential danger. The brain has more blood (and oxygen) and functions very efficiently, discarding irrelevant information in favor of anything related to danger. These reactions are intended to be temporary effects during the alarm phase of a stress response. People who have been traumatized may chronically experience an excessive amount of this activity.

The physical processes that increase and decrease our energy levels are necessary for us to cope with changes in our lives. We experience increased arousal when we perceive a threat or need to take action.

Trauma appears to reset the noradrenaline system, leaving the individual more prone to adrenaline surges that increase one's energy and arousal levels. When confronted with a stressor, the individual experiences a rush of noradrenaline, greatly increasing general arousal. This rush is analogous to pushing the gas pedal all the way to the floor. Some experience a constant rush of noradrenaline, as if their gas pedal is stuck down. This system is involved in modulating the stress response as well as memory encoding, anxiety, and fear. The locus coeruleus, a brain structure that contains 90 percent of the noradrenaline cells, greatly influences the limbic system. This part of the brain is composed of several structures that modulate emotional reactions and, in conjunction with the frontal cortex, is involved in planning and rational decision making. Changes in the locus coeruleus and then the limbic system may result in chronic emotionality.

Other physical effects of trauma also impact the body's physical arousal. For example, the functioning of the hypothalamus and pituitary gland, two brain structures, may be changed by trauma.

These structures trigger the release of CRF (Corticotropin-releasing factor), a hormone released during stress. The oversecretion of CRF results in a decreased number of receptors for CRF, which then increases further CRF secretion. This in turn compounds effects of adrenaline and functionally is related to increased perception or judgment of danger. Fear, terror, avoidance of vulnerability, and thoughts of danger are increased.

Another system modified by trauma is the opiod system, the automatic and natural response to pain. Natural opiods, chemicals released in the brain, impact our experience of painful sensations and emotions. These chemicals function in the same way as other opiates, such as heroin. Exposure to trauma can greatly increase the production of these natural chemicals, resulting in emotional numbness, apathy, and a general lack of interest. Nightmares, nervousness, and mood swings are associated with increased opiod activity. Intense emotionality involving intense expression of anger and fear may be a product of this activity. In addition, high secretion of these chemicals is associated with self-stimulation, risk taking, crisis seeking, and the interpretation of events as dangerous. Some researchers theorize that a traumatized person may become addicted to their own natural opiods and engage in dangerous or stressful crisis behaviors as a means of facilitating the release of these substances. Others self-medicate through the illegal use of narcotics.

Using magnetic resonance imaging (MRI), researchers have also demonstrated that a brain structure involved with memory is physically altered following trauma. Mid-Hippocampal volume, or the size of this brain structure, is actually smaller in chronic PTSD patients compared to healthy subjects. Similar findings have been reported in animal research.

During the last twenty-five years, researchers have linked many of the psychological impairments produced by trauma, such as memory disturbances, flashbacks, nightmares, apathy, emotional numbing, alcohol and substance abuse, and self-stimulating risk taking, with physical, neurophysiological changes. The post-trauma brain may actually function differently than if the trauma had not occurred. Furthermore, the post-trauma brain may actually be altered in size and shape. Following trauma the brain may be more reactive, more emotional, and may generate varied sensory experiences (dreams, flashbacks). Some research findings suggest that trauma experienced during childhood can have lifelong effects on the developing brain, permanently altering how the person thinks, feels, and behaves.

Emotional Reactions

The emotional reactions to trauma are similar in many ways to those of grief, with the same dynamics of shock, fear, hurt, anger, sadness, and shame. There are significant differences in emotional functioning as well. The emotions may function as intended to warn and equip a person to adapt, but excessive emotionality may occur that does not have a functional value but is rather the consequence of neurophysiological dysfunction.

Many traumatized people experience an emotional numbing, as if they have lost their emotions. Their emotional reactions may seem blunted or constricted. Events that used to bring pleasure or disgust now elicit little if any reaction. They may describe their experience as flat, numb, anesthetized.

When confronted with a flashback or intrusive memory, these individuals may experience intense and overwhelming terror, rage, fear, or hurt. At other times, an intense, painful emotion may intrude upon their present experience. The intensity may be much greater than occurred in the original situation and more intense than would be anticipated even with full understanding of the flashback. As previously noted, one of the physical consequences of trauma can be a disregulation of the emotions. As such, the intensity of these emotions is more a factor of neurological dysfunction than a reaction to present or past events.

It is important for the pastoral counselor to be knowledgeable of this phenomena. Traumatized people have had terrible experiences in their past. The present experience and display of emotion is very real to them. However, it often does not indicate something directly about their past or present but rather is a painful byproduct, an indirect consequence of the trauma. Excessive focus on expression of this emotion may only cue further pain. Thus, the pastoral counselor must discern the function of emotional expression and help the individual acquire coping skills for modulating their painful emotions and decreasing their excessive physical arousal.

Thoughts/Beliefs/Cognitive Processes

The thinking processes of traumatized people are initially focused on basic survival and later on adjusting their schemata to the changes. Emotions may inhibit thinking and problem solving. Attempts to ignore the emotional reactions often only strengthen the inhibition.

Congruent with the emotional reactions, concentration and focus of attention is often diminished. The traumatized individual will often experience increased distractibility. One man, many years after the traumatic loss of his wife, spoke of his mind being "stuck in muck."

Some people direct their attention toward those things that are related to the trauma, other people, away from anything even remotely associated. Some obsess on details while others display phobic reactions. Attention is often selective and new events are filtered through this paradigm.

Trauma changes one's worldview. Following such events, trust and hope are often lost or greatly impaired. Faith is challenged. Values change, often with a decreased value of material objects, power, or status and an increased appreciation and desire for relationships. A fast-climbing junior executive who lost his son in a boating accident commented "What does my job really mean? My power and status did nothing for my son except keep me away from him. Now what do I have?"

As with emotions, intrusive thoughts are common for those who have experienced trauma. Without warning, and seemingly out of context, a memory, thought, image, or statement will spring into consciousness, disrupting everything else. These thoughts may not be logical and, for some, involve false accusations of guilt. For others, these thoughts are mental reruns of the traumatic event. Such flashbacks can seem very real, as if the trauma were happening in the present. Not only are the thoughts the same as then, the senses (sights, smell, touch, taste, and hearing) may all be experienced as if the trauma were occurring in the present. It seems too real, as if the trauma is repeated again and again.

Intrusive thoughts and feelings regarding the trauma are not only common but are also a functional and often important part of the *accommodation* process necessary for *adaptation*. In a dynamic process defined by Harowitz (1979), a balance exists between the controls (or defense mechanisms) determining how much emotional pain is experienced and what memories are allowed into awareness. If the controls are inadequate, memories and painful emotions flood and disable the person. In contrast, overcontrol diminishes the person's overall emotional availability and interferes with or inhibits the adjustment process. Harowitz uses the term oscillation to describe the alternating between reliving past trauma and living in present reality.

Perceptions/Sensations

Flashbacks activate internal sensory signals that confuse the person, confusing the past with the present. An intrusive memory of combat trauma, for instance, may be accompanied by the smell of burning wood and flesh. Furthermore, sensory information can cue a flashback. A combat veteran may have a flashback to a battle scene upon hearing a firecracker or a car backfire. A woman who was sexually abused by someone singing nursery rhymes may have a panic attack or flashback upon hearing nursery rhymes in the present.

People who were traumatized over a period of time tend to have sensitivity to many stimuli. Previously neutral or low intensity stimuli, such as humming by another person, may become overwhelming and irritating. Formerly benign events now are perceived as threatening or dangerous. Much of this processing occurs at levels outside of conscious awareness.

Behavior

Many of the behaviors exhibited during and following exposure to trauma are highly correlated with the physical effects of trauma previously discussed. During the trauma physical survival is often paramount. Depending upon the event and the person's coping capacities, the individual may be very passive, coolheaded, aggressive, or even uncharacteristically violent. Later evaluation of how the person behaved during the actual trauma must be done in the context of the need the person had to survive. Whatever the person did to survive, even if it meant another person did not, must be understood in the context of the incredible demands placed on the person at that time and the innate reaction to survive.

Survivors of trauma will often engage in increased scanning of their environment. They are likely to become increasingly aware of what others are doing, where they are in proximity to themselves, and form very quick opinions as to why others are behaving as they are. This hypervigilance is likely to be accompanied by a hyperstartle response. A small, seemingly insignificant event such as someone tapping their fingers on a table may elicit a strong physical and emotional reaction from traumatized people. If surprised they may exhibit an extreme reaction.

Sleep is often impaired. They may have difficulty relaxing enough to enter sleep or they may wake early and they may have dreams of the trauma or in which the trauma is symbolically acted out.

Eating may increase as a means of obtaining satisfaction, soothing, or comforting. For others, eating is diminished in an attempt to reestablish control in their lives. While they were unable to control the trauma and experienced helplessness, they can influence how much they eat or how their body looks. Anorexia or bulimia may result.

Some survivors become very cautious and avoid potentially dangerous situations. This may turn into phobic fears of any potentially dangerous situation and immobilize the person. Or, a person may avoid life through the increased and dangerous use of drugs and alcohol.

Others respond in the opposite manner and engage in risk-taking behaviors. A mother of a girl killed by shelling during the war in Bosnia was found to frequent the parts of town most likely to have active fighting. She wondered "why wasn't I lucky enough to be killed?" A man who lost his family in a fire takes up sky diving and bungee cord jumping. For some, there is an implied wish to die while for others there seems to be an attempt to tempt death, to prove "I'm alive."

Suicidal attempts increase following traumatization. Traumatized people may be able to muster the resources to cope with their initial trauma but reach exhaustion, unable to modify their schemata or replenish their coping resources. Such individuals often use clearly lethal means of suicide: a gun, hanging, or carbon monoxide poisoning. Their suicidal behaviors are attempts at solving the problems of loss of meaning, hope, companionship, and an attempt to obtain freedom from the pain.

Another behavioral response is to aggress against others. The confusion, rage, and hurt can be directed away from the self and toward others in the form of verbal, emotional, sexual, or physical abuse. Unable to reorganize their schemata and regain a sense of personal control, some attempt to dominate or intimidate others. Furthermore, as coping resources are depleted, more primitive behaviors often emerge. Frustration tolerance decreases, irritability increases, and conflict becomes more common and more threatening.

Social Relationships

The emotional and physical arousal subsequent to trauma often prompts people to withdraw, to pull back from others and protect themselves. They may seek less social contacts, turn down invitations to socialize, or, when with others, seem distant, cold, and removed. Relationships may become more superficial.

Fear of being vulnerable often is manifested in those who have experienced trauma. Such fear contributes to social isolation and superficial relationships. Difficulties with vulnerability may also intrude upon one's marriage. Relationships often become strained; sexual relating is often avoided or impaired. The fear may be of letting others know what it is like to be them ("they may think I'm crazy" or "it may hurt them"), or fear of caring for others ("I may lose them"). Feeling for or caring for others may lead them to feel their own feelings.

When trauma has impacted an entire community, such as a flood or high-profile murder, it is common for there to be an initial sense of support, belonging, and unity. Neighbors who had previously been uninvolved lend help and support. There may be a sense of us versus them, those of us who experienced the trauma are united in our common experience and needs in contrast to the outsiders who have not had the experience. As time passes, individual needs appear to become more salient and outweigh common goals. The support that initially bonded the survivors may be depleted. Individuals who had joined together tend to become more focused on meeting their own needs.

Spiritual Experience

All of one's being, all assumptions and understandings, all beliefs and hopes can be challenged by trauma. Our view of God, our relationship with him, and the nature of our earthly existence may all be brought into question. For some, traumatic experiences strengthen their faith as other people, objects, or even beliefs about the self are lost. God alone remains stable. For others, the horror of the trauma, the pain, and seemingly unanswerable questions dissolve their faith. Some pull away from other people as well as from God.

Most trauma survivors will question God as they attempt to modify their schemata. Easy answers, and the answers they had prior to the trauma, are not satisfying. The questions may be attempts to make sense of what has happened and to determine what is real and lasting, or they may be the expression of strong feelings of anger, pain, or hurt. The questions may be a crying out for relief from the entire situation. These questions, which are part of the readjustment, are very often a necessary part of coping.

Vulnerability to Further Trauma

Once a person has experienced trauma, he or she often greatly fears further catastrophe. As one survivor of a major flood put it, "I'll never look at water the same." The trauma has altered the person's schemata in one form or another. Innocence has been lost, a sense of being protected and safe, if ever evident, is now gone. Some report they never again feel the safety and security they once had. Their worldview has been altered.

For some, past trauma serves in a manner analogous to an inoculation. Having had prior exposure to a similar trauma, a person may actually be better equipped to handle the present situation. The experienced combat soldier may be better equipped to respond to an enemy attack than the fresh replacement. Previously acquired coping strategies may be activated and allow for more effective coping.

The effects of trauma are cumulative. As our capacities to cope are finite, we tend to become more vulnerable to the experience of trauma. An event that would have been merely distressing may become traumatic if the individual is depleted or already overwhelmed. While some events would be traumatic for any person, other events are traumatic in relation to the individual's coping capacities.

The timing of subsequent traumas also impacts the experience and capacity to cope. We typically need time following trauma to again acquire *adaptation*. We need multiple experiences to be able to reshape our schemata. Successive traumatic events deplete coping resources and magnify the disorganization and pain.

Coping with Trauma

Trauma overwhelms the person's capacity to cope. Existing schemata are inadequate to account for the external reality and the body's coping capacity is stretched to the limits. Resolution will involve both an adaptation of the schemata to develop a sense of meaning, understanding, and acceptance of the traumatic event and a decrease in basal arousal of the body. The resolution of grief is achieved when mourners adjust to their loss; trauma is resolved when traumatized people adapt their schemata to account for the trauma and develop a capacity to modulate their physical arousal.

The goals of coping with trauma may be best understood in terms of short-term and long-term coping.

Our defense mechanisms may be helpful or harmful to our functioning. Living in a sinful world, we need coping strategies that can be implemented for our protection. At times, we may need to minimize the risks we are facing or have a buffer from the hate and rejection we may encounter. For example, most of us deny the risks involved in driving a car. We would be highly anxious or impaired if we were constantly consciously aware of the risks involved. Our physical arousal would likely be dangerously high. Our defense mechanisms help protect us from this type of awareness and arousal. People may experience overwhelming anxiety if their defense mechanisms are too great or too weak. In such situations, these coping strategies may become rigid, contributing to choices to take unsafe risks or engage in inflexible behavior patterns that may diminish one's anxiety but that may also create difficulties with relating to others, accepting one's self, or being responsive to the environment.

Initially, the individual is focused on survival. What do I need right now? How can I be safe and protected? This is where coping begins.

A soldier under fire in combat is most likely initially to become very still, even frozen, and unable to act. A woman being raped may sense time stand still and feel as if somehow she has become separated from her own body, as if this crime is happening somewhere else. These initial reactions, which are defense strategies or mechanisms, occur automatically. Much like a deer stopping on the road when hit with headlights, humans have various capacities to react automatically for protection. We have been created with the capacity for self-protection. When our capacity to cope is threatened, when our schemata are inadequate to organize and interact with external reality, automatic coping strategies (defense mechanisms) are activated—strategies that are essential for short-term survival. Should these mechanisms be activated excessively, they can actually interfere with long-term coping.

Understanding these defense mechanisms has two advantages. First, for the counselor, they are indications of how the person is coping. What defense mechanisms were activated by the trauma? How did the person survive the experience? These questions can be answered by identifying the defenses. The defense mechanisms serve to solve problems; they help the person to cope. Should the defenses become excessive, the pastoral counselor can continue to understand them as attempts to solve a problem that may lead to alternative strategies for solving the problem. Being able to identify the presence of a defense mechanism provides a description and contributes to understanding of the person's present functioning. This description of the behavior and experience is not a justification for the behavior.

Second, these automatic strategies are amazing, wonderful capacities that help us survive in a sinful world, even when they have become dysfunctional. Accepting the mechanisms can decrease the traumatized person's fears and increase his or her sense of self-control and personal meaning.

High-level defenses that allow the greatest immediate adaptation to external reality include humor, self-observation, suppression, or sublimation. They help people consciously experience their thoughts and feelings and remain present reality oriented.

Mental inhibitions can serve to distance the self from potentially threatening realizations, observations, feelings, sensations, emotions, memories, or fears. A common defense for those who have been traumatized, dissociation, alters the experience of the self. The typical sense of self and psychological functioning of the self as a whole, unified person is disrupted. The integrated functioning of memory, perception, thinking, feeling, and identity are disturbed. This may take many forms. *Dissociative amnesia* results in the inability to recall important personal information associated with a traumatic event, such as a flood survivor who cannot recall how he escaped from a submerged car. *Dissociative fugue* is characterized by an inability to recall one's identity and the establishment of a new identity following a sudden, unexpected move. Such people may disappear from their community and be found only months or years later after they have established a new identity.

Multiple personality disorder, or *dissociative identity disorder*, is also a defense against trauma. The establishment of unique and separate identities with their own memories, feelings, and abilities is an attempt to isolate the part of the self that encountered the trauma. In such cases, each personality state is experienced differently and separately from the others, as if the same body housed several people.

Another common dissociative defense for traumatized persons is *depersonalization disorder* in which they retain an orientation to present reality, but experience a sense of detachment or estrangement from themselves. It is as if they are living in a dream,

watching themselves in a movie, or are outside themselves looking in. Often they feel as if they are not in control of their own
actions or speech, that life is happening to them and they are passive observers. People who witness a loved one being murdered
may detach themselves from the scene, not only in what they
observe but also in what they sense, think, and feel.

Intellectualization, or the use of cognitive processes to guard
against emotions, memories, or insights, and *repression*, the unconscious removal from awareness of unacceptable memories,
thoughts, or feelings are common in coping with trauma. A person
may talk about the trauma but instead of expressing the passion,
emotion, or other personal reactions, he or she sounds like an
objective news reporter. In Dragnet style, he or she may be giving
"just the facts." A pastoral counselor may notice that there are significant details missing in the story, yet, when this is pointed out to
the person, he or she may seem confused or deny any missing
pieces. In the person's experience, there are no gaps.

More primitive defenses, such as *denial, splitting,* and *acting
out* may be activated if other defenses are inadequate or unavailable to the traumatized individual. A person may literally not recognize a stimulus in the environment, denying its presence, as in
the survivor of an auto accident who does not acknowledge that
prior to the accident his or her walking gait was normal and now it
is abnormal. Splitting allows for the evaluations and emotions associated with good and bad to be kept separate. Children who are sexually abused long to believe and feel that their parents are good.
Given the evil of the abuse, they are confronted with a conflict that
does not fit their young schemata. In an attempt to continue to relate
to the parent, on whom they remain dependent, they split and experience a good parent and a bad parent within the same person. Likewise, they experience a good self (which relates to the good parent) and a bad self, the self that was abused. Later in life, they may
have a tendency to organize themselves and others into good selves
and bad selves. They may switch between a caring, positive attitude
toward others and anger and disgust. These individuals often appear
to be unstable in mood, behavior, and relationships.

Acting out can take many forms. Anger often serves to reestablish a sense of personal control or influence in one's life. Having

been victimized and thus put in a powerless, helpless position, survivors may respond by taking definitive actions. They may violate their moral code in anger, use resentments and bitterness to protect themselves from further vulnerability, or engage in risk-taking behaviors. Some almost tempt death itself, seemingly trying to demonstrate that they are now in control.

In a similar manner, some develop *passive-aggressive* features or *apathetic withdrawal*. The attempts to cope with the demands of the stressors involve indirect anger expression or expression of anger against the self. Such people may attempt to cope by withdrawing from everyone, freezing, seeming not to care about others or even about themselves.

Finally, some experience trauma so great and/or their coping capacities are so compromised that they cannot maintain contact with objective reality. For such individuals, the defenses of *delusional projection, psychotic denial,* and *psychotic distortion* occur. Persons with such defensives typically need psychiatric interventions. They often benefit from medication and/or hospitalization.

Long-term coping strategies may be helped or hindered by a person's initial responses. Once physical survival is accomplished, the job of psychological and spiritual survival is undertaken. The focus now switches to coping with the overwhelmed schemata and the apparent inability to derive sense or meaning out of the events. How could this have happened? Why? God, if you are loving and powerful, why did you let this happen? Who am I now? The trauma disorganizes the internal world of traumatized people. Their schemata must be modified so that they can account for what has happened, what has been lost, what is now different. They need to acquire a sense of meaning to it all, to regain a perception of predictability, a sense of influence, mastery, or control in their lives. In addition, they need to have confidence that they can understand how their body reacts to events and what they can do to calm themselves.

Long-term coping may involve a rebuilding of the self, the assumptive world, and one's values and expectations. The traumatized person is challenged to move from a traumatized to a new, normalized life, from victim to survivor.

5

From Victim to Survivor—
Healing beyond Trauma

Victim: "one harmed or killed by another . . ."

Survivor: "to remain alive or in existence . . . to live or persist through."

Through the grace and the truth of God, victims of trauma need not have a lifelong fixated identity as victims, but can become survivors.

People are victimized by the losses encountered in grief and the shocking, painful experiences of trauma. Victimization is the inevitable consequence of living in a sinful world, a world in which we have limited control over what happens to us and to those we love. Events occur that harm us, cause us pain, impact how our bodies function, even how our brains develop. Many of these victimizing circumstances are outside our sphere of control. Within ourselves we cry out that something is wrong, very wrong. The writers of the Psalms frequently lament, asking why the wicked prosper and the righteous suffer. Ultimately, the essence of Christianity rests on the most extreme example of victimization: a righteous, sinless person, the Son of God himself, was sacrificed for the guilty.

We cannot escape victimization; even Jesus Christ allowed himself to be victimized for our redemption.

The challenge for the pastoral counselor is to play some role in assisting those who have been victimized to adjust to the losses and changes, to develop an acceptance and find meaning, to modify their schemata to account for reality, and to help victims modify their identity. Some become stuck, fixated in a victim identity, locked in their anger, confusing things that happened to them with who they are. The pastoral counselor can help such people move from having been victimized (what happened), away from being a victim (a description of a person, an identity), and toward an identity in Christ in the present (real identity).

Three Levels of Victimization

The victimization process is an interaction between external events and the ways a person copes with the events. Often, it is only the internal events, one's thoughts, feelings, expectations, that can be modified. How a situation is interpreted, what is valued, the choices made, and what is accepted or rejected are within the realm of personal influence.

Victimization occurs in a three-stage process (Matsakis, 1992). At each level, the pastoral counselor can assist the person by clarifying what is happening, identifying what is needed, and assisting the person in solving the problems that result from the loss or trauma.

The Shattering of Assumptions

Being confronted with a painful loss, realization, or event shocks our schemata, our symbolic and personal understanding of reality. Little may seem real or make sense. Former beliefs and feelings of safety, trust, and the assumption that "it can't happen to me" are lost. Also lost may be a sense of fairness, the belief that "if I do the right thing I'll be okay." New realizations of being helpless and powerless replace former beliefs of being in control and self-directed. Self-esteem is threatened by the powerlessness and by thoughts of self-blame and feelings of shame. Even one's place among other people may no longer seem the same. What is real? Where do I belong?

Such losses also activate dependency needs. Feeling helpless and vulnerable, many are required (possibly for the first time) to accept help from others. They may report "feeling like a child" or "feeling weak." Acknowledging dependency may result in shame. Rather than depend on God and other people, some turn their dependencies toward their own anger (and do not acknowledge their vulnerability) or to alcohol or other substances.

Secondary Wounding

As if the loss or trauma were not enough, the mourner or traumatized person experiences further consequences of the loss through secondary wounding. Others may not understand the grief process, the need of the mourner to ask questions or express emotions. The loss or trauma was very difficult to survive, yet for some, the aftereffects are as painful and damaging.

Jeff, recently married, regained consciousness in a foreign hospital, confused as to what happened. Only later did he learn that his wife did not survive the accident. He looked forward to returning home, anxious to be around friends and family. The next two years were much harder than he could have anticipated. He was shocked that friends suggested he date again only a few weeks following the funeral. As one put it, "you weren't married very long, you need to get on with your life." Three months after her death it started to sink in with him—she isn't coming back. Yet others around him did not want to talk about this any longer and seemed surprised that he did. Some suggested he must not be grieving appropriately.

Most difficult were the responses he received from his in-laws. Without directly saying so, it seemed that they held him responsible for their daughter's death. He had been driving, although he had no memory of the accident. When he shared how hard it was for him, they responded, "at least you get to go on."

Jeff had lost his wife, the person he desired to share his life and dreams with. What he discovered was that he also lost his confidence in relationships, in the belief that others could know, understand, and accept him. He had never felt so alone.

Secondary wounding takes many forms. Following the loss or trauma, others often distance themselves from the mourner or traumatized person. This occurs for many reasons. Others may be ignorant of what to do and, feeling their own discomfort, do nothing. They may experience distress at the realization of the loss or trauma that may activate their own sense of vulnerability. Rather than confront their own pain and questions, they distance themselves from the one in pain. This distance may be accomplished by disbelief, discounting, denial, or blaming the victim. The thought is: if the painful tragedy is someone else's fault, then I am safe for I will not do what they did to cause this. Such defensive thinking further isolates the person as he or she attempts to preserve at least an illusion of being in control.

Another form of blaming victims is manifested in punishment or humiliation of them, judging them for what has happened to them. The victim of rape who is ridiculed for "being available," the grieving mother who lost her child and is accused of "trying to get attention," or the traumatized person whose symptoms are minimized as "he was always a little crazy" are all examples of secondary wounding.

Many people with the best intentions may contribute to secondary wounding in doing what they think will be helpful. Each of us grieve and cope in our own unique ways. When we anticipate that others will experience an event in the same way we do or we ignore what they are telling us and proceed to try to care for them we risk inflicting secondary wounding. A caring response will require attention to what mourners or traumatized people need at the moment, what is relevant to them now, and an acceptance that they are unique and separate people.

Victim Thinking

Ultimately, the most damaging form of victimization is the acceptance of the victim status, the taking on of the identity or self-description of being a victim. Matsakis commented that the third level, *victim thinking*, "occurs when you internalize the victim status. Even though you are no longer in the original trauma situation, you think and act as if you are still being victimized" (1992, p. 94). The loss or trauma has disturbed their worldview and now they must reconstruct their understanding of reality. When one's loss or trauma disturbs one's worldview, one way to redefine reality is to accept an identity as a victim. The person then interacts with the world from the perspective of being a victim: life is interpreted through this lens. Other people are perpetrators, new events are potential traumas, relationships are too vulnerable and risky because of the potential for loss.

The thinking of the person is altered by accepting this self-definition. Victim thinking colors every experience; the impact on life is extreme. Below are listed some of the beliefs a person who is locked into victim thinking may display.

- Others have power; I am weak.
- I can't change my situation.
- I have to stay angry or someone will take advantage of me.
- I am helpless, powerless.
- I am unlovable.
- I can't trust anyone.
- Life should be fair.
- There is nothing I can do.
- I have to have others' approval or understanding.
- I can't afford to make a mistake.
- People hurt me on purpose.
- I need someone to take care of me.
- I'll be okay if only you . . .
- I can't handle it.
- I'm entitled after what I've been through.
- I'm never going to be able to recover from what has happened.
- I'll never be happy again.
- God loves everyone but me.

Often, such people are not aware of these thoughts or may even deny that they believe them. However, observation of their coping styles and relationships can identify that they are operating through the victim-thinking filter. The pastoral counselor can assist people in identifying the thoughts and beliefs they have accepted and that now govern their lives. Identification of these beliefs is a prerequisite for moving from victim to survivor. However, if they are going to let go of the victim identity, they will need something solid to hold onto, to connect with. Again, the pastoral counselor can be of great help in identifying reality. This will require skill, knowledge, and sensitivity as reactions in either extreme (discounting their experience or blaming the survivor at one end of the continuum and minimizing or reinforcing their victim thinking at the other) can be a form of secondary wounding.

Victimization versus Victim Identity

How does a victim identity develop? How do people progress from experiencing something happening to them to the point of redefining who they are? Why do some encounter a tragedy and cope well, are even strengthened, while others appear to be destroyed? Answers to these complex questions offer the pastoral counselor insight and opportunities to help in rebuilding their shattered schemata.

Development of Victim Thinking and Identity

All of us are vulnerable to momentary victim thinking when confronted with loss. For most, the victim thinking is part of the adjustment process, the trying on of different explanations for what has happened. However, some are more vulnerable than others to becoming stuck in victim thinking, failing to make further adjustments. Unrealistic expectations, beliefs about the world and what will happen to and around us, make us vulnerable to slipping into victim thinking when confronted with a loss. Recall that our schemata, our symbolic representation of our world, serves to help us understand, interact, and make decisions. When the schemata are constructed with unrealistic, false beliefs or expectations, they cannot equip us to live in reality. It would be like a baker attempting to make a new dessert using an auto repair manual. The information available, no matter how familiar, does not fit, does not account for what is happening now. Such beliefs are dysfunctional because they do not function or work in the present situation. Repeating and continually acting on these beliefs will strengthen the perception of helplessness. The resulting distress, disorganization, and pain can be overwhelming.

Some who strive to help those with complaints of having been victimized and who are presently experiencing emotional pain (and possibly PTSD symptoms) may actually reinforce or encourage victim thinking. Wanting to validate the pain of the client's experience, some counselors do not identify the victim thinking patterns. Other counselors may even teach such thinking patterns. For example, one counselor believed that everyone who experienced the death of a loved one should be angry with God. When this counselor encountered someone who was mourning and not expressing anger toward God, the counselor instructed him to do so, believing that the man was repressing his hostility.

In a similar manner, some counselors conclude that a child raised in an alcoholic home, a violent home, or otherwise abusive situation will have a specific set of characteristics. Drs. Steven and Sybil Wolin have termed this way of thinking the *damage model* that they contend "glorifies frailty, it lumps trivial dissatisfactions with serious forms of mental illness, and, worst, it portrays the human condition as a disease" (1993). They have proposed an alternative way of understanding the effects of loss and trauma in what they call the *challenge model*. The Wolins have studied adult nonalcoholic offspring of alcoholic parents and discovered that they have learned to successfully adapt their schemata to account for both the strategies needed to cope inside the home as well as in the larger community. They have learned to challenge victim thinking and live differently than their circumstances would have predicted.

Being aware of unrealistic beliefs and expectations can be a starting point in the adjustment process. Listed below are a sample of some unrealistic, dysfunctional beliefs that may increase one's vulnerability to victim thinking.

- I should never feel hurt, loss, or pain.
- Life should be fair.
- I should be able to protect my children from pain or loss.
- It is wrong to be angry.

- God will give me everything I want.
- God will bless me because I've earned it.
- Others should please me.
- I should please others, and they should inform me that they are pleased with what I do.
- Others should know what I want or need.
- Relationships should be easy, or at least not this hard.
- God has abandoned me if I'm in pain or don't get what I want.
- I should be able to find a rapid solution to my problems.
- Life shouldn't be this hard.

The presence of such beliefs, and others that are similar, increase the probability of victim thinking and the development of a victim identity. Disguised in many forms, these beliefs are common in our culture and, when activated, may give a false sense of power, self-righteousness, and order.

The secondary wounding resulting from abandonment by others, either overtly or covertly, can also increase the likelihood of victim thinking. The disconnection that can occur for so many reasons at this vulnerable time may seem to confirm thoughts and questions congruent with being a victim. For others, acting like a victim may actually be reinforced. Victims tend to be more passive, often nondemanding, and easy to influence or control. A dominant or controlling person may feel more comfortable with someone who has a victim identity. Acceptance and love may seem more available from someone who functions like a victim.

The Shame of Victimization

In addition to the other factors already mentioned, many who experience grief or trauma encounter powerful emotional inhibition that interferes with their ability to change and adjust to the present reality. Shame, the emotion activated when one perceives disconnection, is experienced when one is confronted with a loss. Shame functions to inhibit other emotions and behaviors. This inhibition prompts avoidance, withdrawal, defensive behaviors, acting out, and substance abuse. Also inhibited are alternative ways of thinking, solving problems, and interpreting events. Shame can lock in victim thinking.

We are created with a desire and a need to be connected. Connection involves a meeting of the hearts, an openness and vulnerability, a giving and receiving, a recognition and responsiveness to the other person, and communication that the person is valuable. Connection includes being touched, heard, seen.

Disconnection, or a breaking of contact, relationship, or connection, occurs when someone dies, an opportunity is lost, one violates one's own morals or values, hope or meaning is lost, or one's safety is threatened. Disconnection can occur when one is shamed, humiliated, or exposed by a trauma, such as occurs in a rape. People may feel shame when they are physically limited as they become disconnected from how their body is supposed to function. We are vulnerable to the emotion of shame when our expectations do not correspond with objective reality, when our expectations are disconnected from our experience or what is happening in the present.

We may experience shame when we realize what was lost and our inability to reconnect with the lost object or person. We can also become disconnected within ourselves. Choosing to violate our own morals and values may be a conscious choice; dissociative and splitting defenses occur automatically and without choice. Shame can also occur because both grief and trauma involve the loss of meaning. In such situations the emotion of shame inhibits the functional use of anger, sadness, hurt, and other emotional reactions.

Further shaming may occur in the form of secondary wounding. This form of shame, imposed shame, feels like any other type of shame but is due to the behavior of others. People who are impatient or neglectful, or who otherwise act inappropriately around a mourner may be responsible for the disconnection between them and the mourner. However, it is likely the mourner will feel the shame and unrealistically conclude that he or she is guilty, i.e., responsible for a wrongdoing. The widower who is told "you should be over your wife's death by now" may feel shame caused by the disconnection from an expectation ("finish grieving!") and in the relationship with the person who imposed the shame. (These concepts are more fully developed in another book in this series titled *Encountering Shame and Guilt*, 1994.)

The inhibition resulting from the emotion of shame is congruent with victim thinking and identity. This emotional inhibition makes it very hard for grieving or traumatized people to take risks, to reach out to others. Yet part of them longs to be reconnected with what was lost, the person who has died, or how life used to be before the trauma. But it is not possible, and thus the shame intensifies.

Loss or trauma may lead people to sense that part of themselves has been lost. This, in conjunction with the loss of hope and meaning characteristic with trauma and loss, creates a crisis in identity. Imposed shame further distances people from others while their own expectations, which may have functioned well prior to the trauma, now contribute to further disconnection.

Disconnected people search for something that makes sense, something that "fits," somewhere to connect and define who they are. Resolving the shame is necessary in order to resolve the grief and restructure the schemata. This creates a major problem for the mourning and traumatized. If I can't reconnect with what has been lost, is there any hope? My old worldview no longer works, so who am I?

One way to answer these questions is to embrace the victimization and define reality from this perspective—to make one's central identity "victim." Consider the following argument for the victim identity: Something terrible has happened, I have truly been victimized; what I had is gone; I lost what I had because of the trauma; the only way to make sense of where I am now is to focus on the victimization. From here, it is only a small step to using the victim-thinking filter to interpret all experiences—to become, as it were, a full-time victim.

It appears as though, by embracing a victim identity, reconnection, self-definition, and relief from the emotional pain of the shame is achieved. What is gained is an explanation of what has happened, a worldview that is consistent with having been victimized, a filter through which new events can be understood and expectations developed, a definition of where I fit in with others.

Having felt so helpless, the indirect and ineffective use of anger that often accompanies victim thinking can feel powerful, as if I'm in control. The anger is ineffective in that it does not lead to changing what must be changed to be in reality. Rather, victim thinking can direct anger toward those who are trying to help, toward the innocent, and away from what is actually wrong. Furthermore, victim thinking can facilitate avoidance of risk taking, feeling one's pain, and even adult responsibilities. The regression that may have occurred at the time of loss may become chronic if victim thinking is accepted.

There are, however, significant disadvantages: the loss of self, decreased motivation and initiative, helplessness, vulnerability to depression, anxiety, substance abuse, and relational problems. The anger that may feel powerful is likely to isolate, leaving the person alone in bitterness or surrounded with other angry, resentful, and stuck people. The person expresses more anger, but only ends up angrier. Nothing changes—the person has adopted a schema organized around a victim identity.

Overcoming Victimization

Victim thinking is one way, albeit ineffective and detrimental, to solve the problems of disorganized schemata, loss of meaning, shame, and a sense of helplessness and powerlessness. The distress inherent in victim thinking often prompts a mourner or traumatized person to seek counseling. At such times, counselees may not know what they need, only that they hurt, they feel pain, and they don't like what is happening in their lives.

A pastoral counselor may offer a new perspective, another way in which to interpret their past and present, a reconstructed system for schemata organization. Counselees cannot go back to how things had been and their current way of coping is inadequate (as evidenced by their contact with the counselor). Had their efforts at coping been effective they would not have contacted the counselor. Reconnection is necessary for shame resolution, for release from the emotional inhibition. What is there for connection?

A New Identity

Who I am, what I value, and how I interpret my world and build expectations will forever be different. Rather than allowing an event, the loss or traumatization, to define who I am, I can learn to choose to be a person living in the present who has, in the past, experienced a loss or trauma. The loss or trauma can be interpreted through a filter based on truths greater than a single experience, greater than I am. From this new vantage point I can connect with something bigger than me, facilitating a reconnection within myself. My neurological system may never function again as it had, I may always experience an exaggerated startle response. However, I may also have a new, deeper, more realistic view of reality.

The degree to which one's identity is changed is both a factor of the loss or trauma and one's unique characteristics and coping styles. However, all people experience a change in their self-description when confronted with a significant loss or threat. The loss of identity may not be pathological yet still be very significant in the person's life.

The new identity must be connected with something greater than the loss or trauma. Some truths may be found within the self, others only in the revelation of God and relationship with him.

Resiliency

For many, the outcome resulting from a loss or trauma is a strengthening of their identity, faith, and purpose. Tested by fire, they emerge wiser, stronger, and better adapted to their ever-changing world. While they may carry scars from their wounds, they exhibit a realistic acceptance of the complexities and challenges in life. Their schemata have been stretched, modified, and can now assimilate a far greater range of experiences. They demonstrate resiliency, the ability to recover from illness, change, or misfortune.

One striking biblical example is the Apostle Paul who, while being honest about how difficult his hardships were, could still describe himself, by the grace of God, as a survivor:

[24] Five times I received from the Jews the forty lashes minus one. [25] Three times I was beaten with rods, once I was stoned, three times I was shipwrecked, I spent a night and a day in the open sea, [26] I have been constantly on the move. I have been in danger from rivers, in danger from bandits, in danger from my own countrymen, in danger from Gentiles; in danger in the city, in danger in the country, in danger at sea; and in danger from false brothers. [27] I have labored and toiled and have often gone without sleep; I have known hunger and thirst and have often gone without food; I have been cold and naked.

[7] But we have this treasure in jars of clay to show that this all-surpassing power is from God and not from us. [8] We are hard pressed on every side, but not crushed; perplexed, but not in despair; [9] persecuted, but not abandoned; struck down, but not destroyed. [10] We always carry around in our body the death of Jesus, so that the life of Jesus may also be revealed in our body. [11] For we who are alive are always being given over to death for Jesus' sake, so that his life may be revealed in our mortal body.

(2 Cor. 11:24–27; 4:7–11)

Resiliency is a trait that can be learned. The Wolins, challenged by the findings that the majority of people who are raised in alcoholic homes function well and do not become alcoholic, have studied the successful coping strategies of these individuals. They noted that the losses and traumas did leave their marks but that these scars could be used as strengths. The Wolins (Wolin & Wolin, 1993) outlined seven clusters of resiliencies that are coping strategies, or responses to the challenges presented by losses and traumas.

- Insight: the habit of asking tough questions and giving honest answers.
- Independence: drawing boundaries between yourself and troubled others; keeping emotional and physical distance while satisfying the demands of your conscience.
- Relationships: intimate and fulfilling ties to other people that balance a mature regard for your own needs with empathy; the capacity to give to someone else.

- Initiative: taking charge of problems; exerting control; a taste for stretching and testing yourself in demanding tasks.
- Creativity: imposing order, beauty, and purpose on the chaos of your troubling experiences and painful feelings.
- Humor: finding the comic in the tragic.
- Morality: an informed conscience that extends your wish for a good personal life to all of humankind.

These resiliencies, which are acquired characteristics, develop out of the pain and threat of the losses and trauma.

To adjust to present reality a person needs a source of motivation. One option may be anger, which, if not resolved, will lead away from reality adjustments and toward bitterness. Rigid, stagnant victim thinking will focus on the limitations, the damage that has been done, and the wounds, often delaying or interfering with healing.

A second source of motivation may be healthy pride and appropriate love. Wolin observed that in "challenge model therapy, pride drives the engine of change. In damage model therapy, with its exclusive emphasis on the hurts of the past, shame all too often jams the gears" (1993). This pride may be what is referred to in Galatians 6:4–5, where Paul wrote "Each one should test his own actions. Then he can take pride in himself, without comparing himself to somebody else, for each one should carry his own load." This healthy pride, derived from self-examination before God, striving to see myself as God sees me, can provide motivation and a source of connection that may resolve some of the inhibiting shame.

Reconnection with the Truth

The need to reorganize one's schemata, find meaning in a horrible situation, adjust to what has been lost, and learn to cope with the lasting effects of the loss or trauma motivates some to seek help. Their coping strategies have been inadequate to make the desired changes and they turn to a pastoral counselor for something new, something they missed, can't see, feel, or don't understand.

What can pastoral counselors offer such people? First, they can offer human connection. They can listen, strive to understand what the person's experience is like, and provide feedback. This basic connection can begin the shame resolution process, freeing up the counselee's own coping capacities.

Mere listening and validation is often necessary but not sufficient. Depending on where the person is in his or her readjustment process, mere validation may lead him or her astray from the ultimate goal of adjusting to present reality. For example, if a grieving person is in the anger or depression stage and a counselor provided only validation, the counselee may experience reinforcement for being angry or depressed. Rather than anger being a reaction that leads to change, it may become a strategy for receiving validation and connection, thus shame reduction.

Skills that increase a sense of self-control can be taught. Learning how to reduce the physical arousal or stop repetitive thoughts can soothe the counselee and increase perceptions of self-control and safety.

The pastoral counselor can present hope for connection with something bigger than the counselee's personal experience, greater than what is occurring in the moment. By listening and understanding, the counselor may present truths in a manner that gently stretches the schema, challenges the adaptation process, and facilitates the activation of the counselee's own resources, moving toward an identity based on who the person is in Christ in the present reality.

6

Counseling Grieving and Traumatized People

The lowly he sets on high, and those who mourn are lifted to safety.
—Job 5:11

Blessed are those who mourn, for they will be comforted.
—Matthew 5:4

The Role of the Pastoral Counselor

Grief and trauma are powerful human events, and when a pastoral counselor is drawn into them, his or her role has the potential to take on many different forms—some helpful, others unhelpful, some appropriate, others inappropriate. It is critically important that the pastoral counselor understand his or her own reactions to loss and trauma, to know how those inclinations compare with what is normal and healthy, and to bear that self-awareness in mind when approaching the whirlwind of emotion that often accompanies grief and trauma situations.

Appropriate Roles

The pastoral counselor has the opportunity and the privilege to be a major element of healing when loss or trauma occurs. That is

147

why so many pastors will testify to both the difficulty of dealing with the painful situations of grief, but also the sense that something significant and eternal was accomplished by helping an individual or a family through the frightening darkness of life's losses. At times of loss or trauma the masks and superficialities often get stripped away, the pastoral counselor is faced with people who ordinarily would never cry in front of someone else, but now they do. People often raise personal issues or reveal deep-running personal thoughts and feelings; they become vulnerable in ways that they rarely do.

When they later assume more or less their old roles they will shift away from that vulnerability. There is, then, a moment where the soul is laid open—in some cases just two or three days perhaps, right around a funeral or right after the car accident—a sensitive time when the pastoral counselor must consider his or her responsibility to provide appropriate care and to protect like a surgeon who, looking at a patient laid open on the operating table, knows he must work effectively and guard against infection.

Pastoral counselors must carefully weigh the words that are spoken to a person whose heart has abruptly become exposed to the harsh environment of this world and its fallen inhabitants. As Proverbs indicates, "the tongue has the power of life and death" (Prov. 18:21); and "words aptly spoken are like apples of gold in settings of silver" (Prov. 25:1).

In the face of loss or trauma many people instinctually look for divine comfort. The person who sees a pastor walk into the hospital room or ICU and says "thank goodness you're here," the person who calls the pastor in the first few phone calls he makes after someone has died, those families that pull themselves together and come as a group for Sunday worship even when it hasn't been their pattern—all are examples of the spiritual reaching out of grieving and traumatized people. Of course, there are those who withdraw, but that is more the exception to the rule. One of the greatest mistakes a pastoral counselor can make is to assume that hurting people ordinarily want to be left alone.

To put it another way, the pastoral counselor is letting the mourning or traumatized person borrow strength. It is one person who has slipped or stumbled in the walk of life and has reached out to hold onto someone who has both feet on the ground and can help him or her get stabilized. It is what Paul means in 2 Corinthians 11–13 and numerous other places when it speaks of the complementarity of strength and weakness in healthy Christian communities.

It may not be assumed that every pastoral counselor knows how to lend strength, however. That brings us to two unhelpful stances a counselor may take: underidentification, where a certain aloofness and indifference prevents the counselee from connecting with any strength in the counselor; and overinvolvement, where the counselor becomes too emotionally identified with the counselee and thus has become weakened in the same way that the counselee is.

The Problem of Underidentification (Type 1 Countertransference)

The pastoral counselor is not a neutral entity in the counseling process. The inner responses going on in the counselor as he or she hears the tragic story of an untimely death or the repugnant wickedness of terrible trauma will prompt a response in the counselor that springs from temperament, values, and personal disposition toward issues of loss and grief.

One such reaction is underidentification, called by psychologists countertransference type 1. It is a response of detachment, avoidance, and relative disinterest. The counselor holds the hurting person at arm's length showing little empathy, believing that the best thing that can be done for the hurting person is to move him or her quickly and rationally away from the pain.

The first tactic of such a counselor is to deny or minimize the problem. "Looking on the bright side" may take many different forms: "yes, the doctor has said he thinks you have cancer, but doctors don't know everything"; "are you sure you aren't just imagining or exaggerating in your mind the severe beatings you had as a child?"; "yes, it is sad that you lost a leg in the car accident, but just think, it could have been much worse, you could have been killed."

The pastoral counselor may put up barriers to hearing the story of the counselee. Instead of asking questions to draw out the experience and the emotional state of the counselee, the counselor listens as little as possible and with an air of detachment or even disdain. It's no wonder some hurting people feel rejected, judged, or blamed when they come looking for support and instead get avoidance.

Another response may be to impose unrealisitic expectations of recovery. "Give yourself a few months to grieve your husband's death, but by then you'll want to get back to a normal life"; or "don't you think you're dwelling too much on your child's illness? After all, he's getting the best medical attention he can"; or "I can't believe you've really thought about committing suicide, that doesn't make any sense since you were the one raped, you've obviously done nothing wrong." Such a counselor may offer a minimum of contact, of discussion, and of empathy. He or she may offer pat answers and simple rationalizations.

Where does such a disposition come from? It can be a cultural issue. Some cultures offer and encourage a free expression of grief and mourning, whereas other cultures, for instance northern European, sometimes discourage the vulnerability and weakness of the hurting soul.

But the unempathetic temperament can also spring from personal issues. People who are extremely uncomfortable with their own mortality or who have not properly resolved instances of grief or trauma in their own backgrounds may be inclined to inhibit such expressions in people they counsel. The counselor protects his or her comfort level by regulating and limiting the connection between him or her and the counselee.

The Problem of Overidentification (Type 2 Countertransference)

There is another reaction to the deeply hurting person that is the polar opposite of the underidentification of countertransference type 1. Recent research into what happens to counselors who deal with traumatized persons shows that it is very common for counselors to develop a powerful and influential emotional reaction within themselves that causes them to overidentify with their counselees. Some counselors are so naturally empathetic (which is the strength that they bring to their counseling), that they quickly feel the pain and shock of the stories they listen to.

It is possible to be overly empathetic. If the pastoral counselor finds that the counseling situation becomes personally disruptive, that line may have been crossed. For instance, a pastoral counselor, hearing all the details of a robbery and assault, begins to experience all the feelings of insecurity and fear that the counselee is going through. He doesn't realize at first that it is unusual for him to check the locks on the doors repeatedly, or to have a hard time falling asleep because of the graphic scenes flashing through his head; but when he begins to have a sense of dread at seeing the counselee again, a colleague finally points out to him that he may be in over his head.

The point here is not that the pastoral counselor should never feel the cost of helping the hurting. It is not uncommon, and certainly not inappropriate, for a pastor to choke up at the funeral he is conducting because he himself feels the loss. Rather, the point is that if the pastoral counselor so identifies with the hurting person that he becomes less effective in helping that hurting person, then everybody has lost something.

Grief is not "solved" by someone replacing something or someone who was lost. The pastoral counselor can give a great deal—personal presence, empathy, a solid footing in God's truth, to name but a few—but he or she should never be lured into thinking he or she can replace a loss. In the case of bereavement after death, those who grieve long only for one thing: to have back the one who was pulled past the curtain of death and out of their reach. Pastoral counsel can never replace a person; its aim is to offer comfort and presence as part of the adjustment process.

One of the most disturbing casualties that can happen in the local church is personal, sometimes sexual, misconduct among the clergy. One of the most common scenarios where a pastor becomes inappropriately involved in the life of a counselee is where the profound neediness of a hurting counselee meets with a deep need-to-be-needed in the pastor. The exposed soul of the counselee opens the possibility of a deeply personal intimate bond to be forged unless the pastoral counselor maintains objectivity as to his role. Short-term structured counseling makes such a circumstance less likely than when pastors do long-term counseling; nevertheless, the pastoral counselor needs some means of checking out whether an intense counseling situation is affecting him or her. Any pastor who does a significant amount of counseling ought to seek relationships with peers that can provide a free exchange of advice and accountability.

The Role of Others

Whether desirable or not, helpful or not, other people will be involved in the process of helping the grieving or traumatized person. The pastoral counselor will often find himself or herself having to give advice as to when the hurting person should have contact with other people. Allies in the helping process are crucial, but there may also be times when the hurting person needs some insulation from people or situations that are more harmful than beneficial.

On the positive side, the pastoral counselor should encourage positive, constructive contacts with people who are in a position to show empathy and walk with the hurting person through the valley of pain. If the counselee refers to a parent, a spouse, or a friend in appreciative ways, when it is obvious that these people are a refuge and a shelter, then the pastoral counselor should suggest ways in which the counselee can appropriately lean on these agents of love and mercy. The person suffering severe loss or trauma needs more than just the pastoral counselor. More than anything, he or she will benefit from the consistent presence of a network of family and friends who can escort the bereaved person through the difficult passages of adjustment, reevaluation, and change.

Unfortunately, there are many people who have no contact with supportive family and friends. There may be one person who really understands and who is willing to stick with the person through the process of adjustment. The pastoral counselor should encourage the counselee to turn to that person in ways that are appropriate and with reasonable expectations on the part of the counselee.

Sometimes the pastoral counselor will have to play a protective role. Many grieving or traumatized people have contact with family and friends, many of whom mean well, but have little understanding of the dynamics of mourning and so offer detrimental advice. A young wife dies, leaving a young husband and two preschool children. Everyone is searching for the meaning of it all and searching for words that will help the unexpecting young widower. Someone will suggest that she is in a better state and is happier than ever in earthly life, which may be true, but it is not a "solution" that will move the husband out of what may be the most desperate moment in his life. Someone else focuses on the heart-wrenching needs of the children, but altogether ignores the grief of the husband who, it is assumed, cannot have personal needs in the light of his children's greater needs. There may even be those who have already figured out who can be the husband's next spouse—perhaps a volunteer has been arranged among the friends of the deceased. To replace a lost wife with a new one, however, just looks like a weak reflection of the parent who quickly finds a new puppy to replace Spot who was taken away by a speeding car.

Often counselees will mention such incidents and passing comments to the pastoral counselor, and even if they don't ask directly, what is on their minds are evaluative questions: Is what this person told me right? Is this supposed to make me happy now? How am I going to deal with people who expect me to bounce back more quickly than I'm able? Is there something wrong with me that I don't find comfort in their words?

The counselor is an interpreter. He or she may need to assure the hurting person that the hollow feeling of grief is normal, not shameful; that he or she does not need to take care of others who have a more distant relationship with the loss; that the stabbing pain felt at the loss, and the ongoing stabs that come all during the day or in the middle of the night, issue from the value or love that was part of the relationship now lost. The counselor may need to steer the counselee toward the people who have love to offer and away from those who inflict further injury.

The church ought to be a place where hurting people can be referred. Sometimes it is, and sometimes it isn't. Where there are previous connections with loving people the counselee should be encouraged to be responsive to the outreach of those people at a time of crisis or loss, while retaining the right to be able to say, "I really appreciate what you are trying to do for me now, but I can only handle so much contact these days." It is obviously not good for the grieving or traumatized person to withdraw into isolation; but neither is it healthy for him or her to feel obligated to entertain acts of mercy even to the point of exhaustion.

What Grieving People Don't Need

We have already touched on many of these issues, but because they are so important let us summarize the mistakes that can make for ineffectual or even detrimental counsel for the mourning and the traumatized.

Withdrawal

One of the most common mistakes even well-meaning people make is to assume that the way to be helpful to the grieving person is to help him or her think of something else. The last thing you do is to directly bring up the loss, for (it is assumed) if the person remembers again his or her loss, it will be pain added to pain. In point of fact, under normal circumstances, the grieving person probably recalls his or her loss all the time. A widow who lost her husband three years ago may still have a rush of grief when she enters the restaurant that was her husband's favorite and smells his favorite foods, or when she passes the exit on the freeway that he used to take to his office, or cleans the bookshelf containing his favorite books. She may want nothing more than for someone to reminisce with her about her lost husband, to bring out warm memories, to choke up with tears if it happens—anything but the convenient and cold suppression of the memories of the lost. One of the best ways for a person to come to terms with loss is to be able to validate the living memory and ongoing significance of the person who was lost.

Many people withdraw from grieving people because they are afraid they may say the wrong thing. They believe that they may inflict injury by their presence when the greater injury will occur with their abandonment. If a pastoral counselor can offer anything self-sacrificially it is the personal comfort that will, and must, be sacrificed in order to hear the sad song of the mourner.

Criticism

It seems so obvious that grieving or traumatized people should not be criticized for their situation, and yet because it does happen, it must be mentioned. It may not be overt, and those putting out the criticism may not be aware of what they are doing. After a serious auto accident people will have many questions, some of which are subtly indicting of the victim: "I've been thinking you haven't been getting as much sleep as you ought to," or "do you think you were driving too fast for conditions?" or "remember how I told you that you really ought to be driving a safer car?" or "I know I wouldn't drive down there during rush hour." The person whose spouse suddenly died of a treatable disease: "Why didn't you take him to the doctor sooner?" or "You just can't fool around with general practitioners, he should have gone to a specialist." The examples abound.

The pastoral counselor is presumably sensitive enough not to be critical of the grieving or traumatized counselee; nevertheless, he or she should be aware that the ethical and moral dilemmas that pain and suffering raise may dispose any spiritual leader to process the event by assessing blame. Even in the situation where the survivor does bear some culpability, the process of dealing with guilt does not necessarily precede the process of grief (the mother whose baby was kidnapped when she left him in the shopping cart; the person who carelessly ran a red light and whose friend is killed when the car is broadsided; the person who convinced his friend not to go to the hospital for chest pain, and the friend dies).

One subtle form of criticism can be evaluation and comparison that happens all the time. A couple privately grieves their inability to have a second child, and when they do express their grief they hear exactly what they were afraid of: "you certainly can be grateful for the one child God did give you." There is the common "it could have been worse" sort of counsel: "Yes, you do have disfigurement to deal with, but at least you're alive." "It's a tragedy that your baby was lost in the fire, but at least your other two kids made it out alive." "The rape must have been awful, but you can be grateful that you didn't end up pregnant."

It is not that the "it could have been worse" line of reasoning is untrue, and indeed, some counselees themselves raise the point repeatedly. There may come a point when what did happen and what could have happened inspires the person to change his or her values or lifestyle. The point here, rather, is that the "it could have been worse" line is not the "solution" to the "problem" of grief. When grief occurs it is the signal that a loss has occurred, which must be realized by being felt so that a new reality can be adopted and personal adjustments made. In other words, the unreal hypothesis of what *might* have happened may be a diversion from the person facing squarely what did happen.

Platitudes or Quick Fixes

The believing Christian counselor knows that there are words that can give life—but they are different from platitudes. We also know that there is healing that can come after loss or trauma, that there can be significant turning points in the process—but that this is different from quick fixes.

A platitude is a trite statement expressed as if it were original or significant. The platitudinous use of the Scriptures should be avoided at all costs. The meaning of Romans 8:28, "in all things God works for the good of those who love him" has often been twisted into the following shape: God is good, God works all things together for the good, therefore everything that happens must be good in some sense and you should try to see the good things that are going to come out of this loss. But that is not what the verse says, which is, that God (because he is good) works toward the good and that he is doing so at all times under all circumstances ("in all things"). Murder is not a good thing, neither is cancer, adultery, starvation and impoverishment, enmity, or unemployment. The grieving person does not have to translate a woeful loss into something good. Yet he or she can be assured that a sovereign God takes all circumstances under the sun, losses as well as gains, and is able to continue to work goodness into the lives of those he loves. Most people who have lost something or someone valuable will agree that it is better to have loved and lost than to have never loved at all—and that's no platitude.

Some Christians seek a quick fix to trauma or grief because they think the gospel of Christ will somehow seem insufficient if it cannot deliver a speedy recovery (although certainly the real issue is often the common human desire to avoid pain). But what makes us think God prefers immediacy to process? The entire Christian life is one of growth and development—so also the hard, educative process of rearranging one's life to adapt to a significant loss. Our reactions to trauma and grief are some of the most profoundly maturing processes that anyone can experience. No wonder it takes time.

This does not preclude decisive experiences such as the flash of insight, the turning point, the moment of catharsis, the new resolution. All these may happen as part of the process of grieving, but they are still part of a process.

What Grieving People Do Need

The Gospel of John tells us that Jesus came, "full of grace and truth." This powerful pair of gifts could define almost any form of Christian counseling, but especially when dealing with grieving people. Grace is given when the counselor offers patience and understanding, practical assistance, and personal presence; truth is given when the counselor becomes a touchstone of reality for a person who may be thrown into confusion or abject despair.

Reflection of Reality

We'll begin with truth. There is a hard reality that the mourner needs to come to terms with, and that reality is part of the truth. In the time immediately following a sudden loss there may be a numbness in the bereaved, an ongoing sense of shock at what has happened. Many people will say that they find themselves sometimes imagining they are awakening after a bad dream. The death of spouse, parent, or child, for instance seems unreal—it is not the way the architecture of their lives has been lived. Thus it is not just the insult of death or its ugly face that stuns the bereaved, it is the removal of a whole part of life, like taking one leg away from a table or taking away one of your senses.

Defense mechanisms like denial can be a short-term blessing. In the same way that a physician may use local anesthetic to dull the senses while the flesh is being traumatized, it seems as though God has made the human psyche capable of numbing itself until the trauma of sudden loss can be dealt with.

The pastoral counselor is thus in a position of having to reflect reality back to grief-stricken people while protecting the necessity that they sometimes have to adjust to that reality step by step. One of the few rituals of mourning still retained by many is the funeral and preparations for it as guided by a pastor. While viewing the body of the deceased cannot be forced on the bereaved, the pastor certainly can encourage it so that the bereaved can face the reality of the loss. Stories abound of people for whom the reality of the death of a loved one is still something of a fiction because they avoided the funeral rites; on the other hand, if a pastor meets the family at the funeral home just prior to their viewing the body of the deceased they will likely be comforted. That moment can be a hushed and deeply private time of contemplation about the deceased, or a point of catharsis. In either case they have a kind of interaction with the deceased, but different than before because now only one party can communicate. Oftentimes the family feels some relief after those first moments have passed, and are more capable than they had previously thought of interacting with family and friends who come to pay their respects.

The very fact of meeting with a pastor can bring home the reality of loss to the bereaved. The pastor must discern the inclinations of the mourner. He or she may want to talk about what or who was lost, reminiscing about good times or bad times; or about the event of loss, e.g., how the accident happened, or how the bankruptcy occurred. Any talk based on reality will be helpful.

Once again it must be mentioned that it will be unhelpful to try to help someone by minimizing the loss, for that is not reality. If the bereaved feels slain by the loss, that is part of the reality of the situation. The counselor may know that with the passage of time the bereaved will be able to go on and to do things he or she feels entirely incapable of now, and assurances can be given of what lies ahead; but what cannot happen is for the pastoral counselor to transport the bereaved into that new, rearranged world. The pastor may be there at various points along that process, but it will proceed step by step.

Personal Presence

If pastoral counseling is a ministry of grace and truth then it may be said that grace begins with the simple offering of personal presence. Again and again God tells his people (Old Testament and New) of his perpetual presence. It can hardly be stressed enough how helpful it can be for a mourner to have a compassionate counselor to just be there. If a pastoral counselor is by temperament highly relational he or she may know this instinctually. If, on the other hand, he or she is task-oriented and given to looking for a course of action to solve any problem, there may be a tendency to try to fix the grief or to underestimate the importance of personal presence.

Many grieving people attest to the experience of having people avoid them or be visibly uncomfortable around them. Afraid that they may say the wrong thing, they opt to say very little at all. Once the obligatory consolations are out of the way they change the subject. They may believe that the worst thing that could happen is to remind the grieving person of the loss, which betrays a certain myth: the idea that grieving people are using all their energy to avoid thinking of the loss. In fact, the mourner very often would like nothing better than for someone to raise a question about the friend whose funeral they just attended, or the marriage that is being demolished in divorce court, or the deep longing to have children when none are forthcoming. The loss is a reality one way or the other; talking about it may bring tears, but that does not mean the pain has increased. Most often, talk about the loss decreases the personal pain.

In the office of the pastoral counselor the grieving person may or may not be verbal about the loss. It is not the counselor's role to try to compel the person to talk. It is not the amount of talk that occurs that defines effective counsel. The counselee will benefit just from the knowledge of someone willing to be there for him or her; to be one fixed point when life's circumstances seem to be shifting faster than he or she can keep up with.

Understanding and Patience

Grieving people feel as though no one can possibly know how they feel, and, in one sense, that is true. No one else was the mother of *this* child, or the husband of *this* wife, or the person who was fired from *this* job. The counselor doesn't need to pretend to comprehend the depth and shape of the grief of the counselee in this particular moment; however, the counselor can offer an understanding and appreciation of loss without evaluation or comparison. Having an understanding of the way grief works is most important (cf. chapter 3).

For the pastoral counselor to show patience toward grieving counselees grants them the freedom they need to let the process of mourning work its way out. This means the pastoral counselor avoids imposing expectations on the counselee, or giving guarantees about how the process of mourning will work its way out.

One of the most common concerns of grieving people is the issue of duration: How long will I feel this way? It's been a whole year, why am I not over it yet? Do I have a lack of faith? Why am I still sad about my husband's death even though everyone around me is telling me he is better off now?

Pastoral counselors need to be careful of being impatient themselves with long-term grieving. The mourner's friends and family may get worn down. Someone will come along and suggest that what the mourner needs is a good swift kick to get back to reality. The pastoral counselor finds himself or herself disappointed that the counselee seems sadder or more depressed now than several months earlier. Everyone wants the mourner to feel more relief from the grief, and yet, it will not happen by force.

The pastoral counselor may wonder if the time for understanding is over and if a time of confrontation should begin. Such an artificial choice is unnecessary, however, if the pastoral counselor has been reflecting both love and truth to the counselee from the start. The only way that an unhelpful pampering or overindulgence will have occurred is if the counselor has misrepresented reality to the counselee.

Practical Assistance

Grieving people who are adjusting to a new and perhaps unexpected loss frequently have great gaps that open up in the fabric of their lives. A new widow who has no idea where the bank accounts are or how to decide whether she can continue to live in the same house; a young family is suddenly thrown into confusion when the mother ends up in a months-long coma in the hospital; fire takes away the home of a family and they suddenly find themselves living in a motel. Each of these situations involves the emotional wrenching that comes from significant loss, and added to that, practical difficulties.

The pastoral counselor has a responsibility to the soul of grieving and traumatized persons, but can also be the agent to finding practical resources in times of distressing loss (see James 1:27: "Religion that God our Father accepts as pure and faultless is this: to look after orphans and widows in their distress"). This too is a spiritual ministry in that the grieving person years hence may very well recall that a pastor not only told them that God was there, but that the pastor was there too with words of comfort and acts of mercy. The pastoral counselor may be able to find someone in the church who can provide or organize people who can provide such things as

- meals
- babysitting
- driving
- cleaning
- shopping
- yard work
- making of difficult phone calls
- handling of correspondence and bills
- finding a doctor
- financial advice

How much help is enough? Is it possible to be too helpful? It would be nice if everyone used common sense in answering those questions, but often that is not the case. The pastoral counselor may locate helpers for the grieving, but may sometimes have to help the mourner handle the helpers. Some well-meaning people will impose themselves on the mourner; assuming, for instance, that the husband wants a constant vigil of his wife's friends at her sickbed or surrogate mothers for their children. The pastoral counselor should encourage the counselee to determine what is helpful and what is not, and to feel very comfortable communicating that frankly to the helpers. Some mourners have a hard time telling well-meaning helpers what to do; but they do not need one complication added on top of everything else they are experiencing. Crises often inspire people who need-to-be-needed to have an instant-made role.

The opposite problem often arises as well, where the person experiencing loss is almost abandoned by friends. If appropriate, the pastoral counselor may want to encourage or instruct a close friend on how he or she can be helpful.

The Right Counsel for the Right Time

The experience of the grieving person varies greatly according to the phases of the process (see chapter 3), and pastoral counsel that is given must be applied appropriately according to the phase. It would be a mistake, for instance, to try to force an adaptation to a new world a week after a funeral following an unexpected death; and so also would a counselor be mistaken to counsel a person who is still troubled by grief twenty years after a death as if it happened yesterday. The last portion of this book is devoted to a case study that will illustrate the different forms of counsel. The following considerations apply to the counselor using the three-fold phases of Rando:

AVOIDANCE PHASE

- Remember that denial may be a God-given defense reaction, especially in cases of severe shock due to loss or trauma.

- The pastoral counselor has a duty to reflect reality to the counselee, while being sensitive to how much of the harsher parts of reality the counselee is able to bear early on.
- If the grieving person is experiencing outbursts of anger, or waves of sorrow or fear, the pastoral counselor can assure the counselee of how common those reactions are; that they are not problematic in and of themselves; and that they will settle down over time.
- The grieving person may need from the pastoral counselor a sense of assurance or safety about how to face the loss. For instance, one common question is: "do you think, pastor, we should have a closed or open casket?"

CONFRONTATION PHASE

- The counselor has to be aware that a sense of shock or numbness may come and go. Some of the greatest pain can come months after a loss.
- The pastoral counselor may be one of the safer people with whom the mourner can recollect and reexperience his or her life before the loss, and thus validate the prior existence.
- As the mourner relinquishes old attachments and leaves behind a world that was different before the loss, he or she may need comfort and understanding about the pain of all the secondary losses. Selling a house after a divorce, quitting a couple's bridge club after a spouse dies, getting a smaller car after a bankruptcy, giving away the toys of a deceased child—all are potentially painful steps in the grieving process that may strike other people as no big deal.

ACCOMMODATION PHASE

- As the grieving person adapts to a new world he or she will face many decisions, some of which will shape the rest of his or her life. The pastoral counselor may be in a position to help the person evaluate those decisions so that, for instance, a widower doesn't make a snap decision and remarry into an unviable relationship.
- The pastoral counselor can highlight the positive possibilities for the future life of the mourner (an action not suited

for the Avoidance Phase). Losing one thing doesn't always equate into getting something else, and, as has been pointed out, accommodation does not mean replacement; but any good possibility that does lie ahead should be described in constructive, optimistic terms.

- The pastoral counselor can give hope. Some people just need to keep hearing that there is hope.

Special Considerations When Counseling Traumatized People

People who have experienced trauma present special concerns for the pastoral counselor. All of the considerations regarding counseling those who grieve are relevant. In addition, the unique physical and psychological factors associated with trauma merit additional attention. A knowledge of these challenges can increase the counselor's sense of purpose, security, and effectiveness and will make it possible to offer traumatized people choices and options that may address their fears, sense of powerlessness, and striving for meaning.

Secondary Trauma

The shocking events of trauma are overwhelming, leaving people negatively impacted (often chronically), and also impact those who help the traumatized. Hearing of great loss, pain, torture, terror, or mutilation affects the listener's own senses of vulnerability and safety. Just as one's body, focus of attention, and memory may react following the viewing of an action movie or a powerful drama, the exposure to the stories and expressions of the traumatized impact the listener.

This effect, often referred to as secondary trauma, can produce emotional, physical, intellectual, and relational consequences similar to those produced by the initial trauma. While the intensity of these symptoms are likely to be much less than in the traumatized person, they may inhibit the counselor. This is especially true when a counselor works with many traumatized people. The cumulative effects of being exposed to so many stories of trauma can impact how one perceives one's self, others, the world, and God.

Pastoral counselors who are aware of this potential source of traumatization need not avoid those who have been traumatized. Rather, they can choose to take care of their own needs, to tell their stories to safe people, and to experience a full and balanced life outside of their work. It is very important that the counselor who works with traumatized people have someone safe with whom they can debrief, can consult with, connect with in their reactions to the other's stories, can test reality with, and can tell their own stories to. This is not a luxury but a necessity. The limits of confidentiality, for both the client as well as the pastoral counselor, must be adhered to by all involved.

Ignoring the impact of secondary trauma can lead to burnout, increased countertransference, and violation of boundaries. If we are to be appropriately available to help others we need to be aware of how being exposed to the trauma of others affects us.

The Necessity of Safety

Trauma steals the victimized person's sense of well-being, security, predictability, and safety. Before risks can be taken in counseling, such as learning again to trust or coming close to another person, safety must be established. This can be accomplished by defining and clarifying expectations and boundaries within the counseling relationship, defining and guarding confidentiality, and providing both sufficient feedback to counselees so that they know they are being understood, and sufficient structure to the counseling relationship so that they can sense that the pastoral counselor knows where they are going. Connection with reality and references to the ultimate truth of God can further establish safety. A balance must be struck between responding to the present needs of the traumatized person, maintaining boundaries, and focusing on goals. This balance is the foundation for safety.

Strategies for Residual Physical Effects of Trauma

Trauma may leave one with chronic physical symptoms, changes in how the body functions. These symptoms are not imagined; certain parts of the brain no longer function as they had prior to the trauma. These resulting physical changes can be very scary to the traumatized person and may significantly contribute to victim thinking. For many traumatized people, the physical changes resulting from trauma leave them feeling afraid, alone, helpless, out of control, or very odd.

Providing an explanation, some reason for the symptoms, can provide significant relief of a person's distress and aid in both the acceptance of the symptoms and an increased sense of control in one's life. Basic education regarding the physical effects of exposure to trauma may greatly assist them in self-acceptance. Just knowing that "I'm not going crazy," that it's not "all in my mind" but actually does involve physical changes can be comforting.

With such an understanding, people can then choose to use coping strategies so that they may decrease or eliminate the impact the physical symptoms have in their lives. The initial strategy, *cognitive reframing*, is occurring throughout the educational process. Traumatized people can come to understand that their hyperarousal, hyperstartle response, or hyperemotionality is linked to actual changes in the brain. As such, their arousal and emotional reactions may not mean they are in danger. Rather, they may come to accept that now they have a tendency to overreact. If we rate our reaction intensity to any event on a 10-point scale, with one being a minimal reaction and ten being the most extreme, then prior to the trauma, people may have reacted to being surprised by someone coming up behind them and startling them with an intensity of three. Following trauma, the same startling event evokes a reaction intensity of eight. Cognitive reframing involves adjusting the schema so that they interpret their reactions differently than they did prior to the trauma.

A second general set of coping options, the many relaxation strategies, can further strengthen one's coping abilities. Relaxation, or a reduction in the mental and muscular tension in the body, can be achieved in many ways. Listening to soothing music, remembering or imagining a peaceful place while relaxing in a chair, focusing attention on things that are good and pure while letting muscles feel calm and heavy, or meditating on a psalm or a biblical truth can all contribute to decreasing one's physical arousal. Learning to breathe deeply, using the diaphragm rather than the rapid, shallow breathing resulting from the muscles of the rib cage, can also decrease physical arousal and increase relaxation.

The benefits of learning to relax are many. Relaxation can increase one's sense of control, can calm the emotions and interrupt untrue or troubling thoughts, and can increase one's sense of choice. There are many ways to learn to relax. Pastoral counselors should know how to relax themselves, and acquire a few relaxation options they can offer others.

The extreme emotional reactions sometimes displayed by those who have been traumatized may be very confusing to the counselor. In the nontraumatized person, emotions function to signal or cue changes, but trauma interferes with the signal value of emotions. For example, on a scale of one to ten the fear of a child being injured may have previously been a three but elicits far greater fear, a seven, following trauma. In other words, trauma can amplify overall emotional intensity, thus confusing the meaning of the emotion.

The pastoral counselor should try to provide counselees with a new perspective on why they have such extreme reactions to their ordinary life experiences—why they seem to go from crisis to crisis or seem overwhelmed by normal events. What will *not* be helpful is for the pastoral counselor to engage in a similar level of emotionality or to suspend his or her sense of judgment and objectivity.

The extreme feelings can be addressed and resolved in many ways. Some benefit from expressing anger or pain by hitting a safe object, such as a pillow, until the physical energy is discharged in a way that is not destructive. Others benefit from writing in a journal or being able to tell another person what they are feeling. Often the cognitive reframing cannot occur until the emotions have been expressed. The expression is not the end goal but is often necessary toward reaching the goal of adjustment and acceptance.

Flashbacks, the reliving of traumatic events, also contribute to terror, helplessness, and anxiety. Some flashbacks are triggered by specific events. Identifying the triggers, or events that cue flashbacks, may help decrease their intensity and can increase the person's sense of control and choices in life. Another strategy, *grounding*, can help one remain focused on present reality during a flashback. This strategy involves the person establishing a link between momentary experience and something tangible that allows him or her to focus on present reality. For example, when one begins to feel intense fear and abandonment, one may push one's foot hard on the floor, noting that the floor is solid and stable; it does not give way (abandon the person). Then the person can contact someone safe and have interpersonal connection. Or if becoming highly anxious when in a group, the person may grasp the hand of a spouse or friend, recognizing that they are connected. Grounding actions can disrupt a developing chain of events and can be followed by a relaxation exercise.

For many, the emotion of shame keeps the trauma current. They may blame themselves (think they are guilty) or otherwise judge themselves as shameful. It is helpful to use cognitive reframing to sort out the issues of guilt, to realistically attribute responsibility. In doing so, responsibility must be released where it does not belong and attached where it does. This process of attribution is necessary for the beginning of forgiveness, for one cannot forgive one's self for the wrongs of another.

The emotional reaction of shame is a result of a disconnection. Thus, the pastoral counselor can help the traumatized person reframe his or her shame experiences as manifestations of disconnection. Choice then becomes available as the counselor can help the person identify how and where connection is available.

The worldview of the counselor will impact the direction of the process and the eventual adjustments made by the traumatized person. The pastoral counselor needs to be aware of the knowledge we have gained about the effects of trauma as well as the larger issues of meaning and values. Working with traumatized people will challenge the counselor's own worldview.

When to Refer

It is appropriate to refer to a more experienced or specialized professional under many circumstances, most typically when the pastoral counselor does not have the expertise, resources, or personal capacity to respond to the needs presented by the person. For many pastors, counseling is only one of many ministry responsibilities. A traumatized person may have profound needs—far more than a pastor can meet.

The complexity of the symptoms resulting from trauma may tax the expertise of the "generalist" counselor. Significant disturbances in reality testing, for example, may require specialized therapeutic skills. Furthermore, physical symptoms may be reduced or eliminated through medical treatments.

Pastoral counselors need other colleagues with whom they can share and consult. Questions regarding referral can be explored with such colleagues.

When a referral is appropriate the pastoral counselor may remain involved with the traumatized person. Many pastors will continue to minister to the individual in other aspects of a church program. For others, specific needs and symptoms may be addressed with another professional while the questions of meaning and spirituality can be explored with the pastoral counselor. Communication between the pastoral counselor and the referral professional can be obtained upon consent of the traumatized person. Support, encouragement, and ongoing prayer may be offered by the pastoral counselor in conjunction with other professional services.

$$7$$

Session 1—
The Encounter Stage

The remaining portion of this book is dedicated to a case study that will illustrate the issues raised in earlier chapters about the dynamics of the experiences of grief and trauma, and the role of the pastoral counselor in dealing with them in short-term, structured counseling. In the following example the pastor has occasion to see a grieving couple on five different occasions over a period of seven months following the death of their teenage daughter.

Session 1

Pastor Ed Reid met in his office with Jan and Mark Jacobson late in the morning after the shocking events of the previous evening—their 17-year-old daughter Karen had been killed when she hit a tree alongside a county highway. Her younger brother Jack was in the front passenger seat and sustained a broken leg and various lacerations.

Pastor Reid had seen the family in the hospital in the middle of the night, but the parents were so much in shock that there was little opportunity to talk. The pastor sat with the family as the father tried to console the mother, and he prayed with them before their doctor sent them all home with some sedatives for Mrs. Jacobson. Mark Jacobson asked Pastor Reid if they could see him in the morning when they were thinking a little more clearly.

What the pastor was able to ascertain about the story, mostly from the younger brother, was that Karen had been getting sleepy, was finding it hard to stay awake; and yet, because they were within ten miles of home, kept pushing herself. The car simply took a long veering turn off the highway and the next thing Jack remembered was waking up with the car's dashboard pushed up near his lap, the windshield hanging in large broken pieces, the branch of a tree poking through where the rearview mirror was, and the sight of his sister, slumped to the side, her face badly cut and clothes soaked in a great deal of blood.

Commentary: Ed is at risk of secondary trauma, or the consequences of hearing about the trauma and being exposed to the after-effects of the loss. Pastoral counselors who serve those who are grieving or traumatized will be confronted with their own needs to adjust and cope with what they encounter, as well as to assist others. In this situation, his strong personal reactions indicated to him that this would likely be a very complicated situation. In addition to recognizing his own reactions, Ed observed that Mark and Jan were in shock, that they were not able to assimilate new information. He chose to show love and caring, not attempting to deal with matters of substance but rather showing love. It is not uncommon for healthcare professionals to note the grieving needs of a woman while minimizing or ignoring the needs of a man. In some situations, women are overmedicated while men are ignored.

Pastor Reid had a hard time going back to sleep that night. When the Jacobsons came to his office the next morning he was already feeling drained. The Jacobsons walked slowly into his office, Mark with his arm around Jan, helping her into her chair. Her gaze was slightly down as if she were in a different world. Mark immediately spoke up:

"Thanks so much for coming to the hospital last night, pastor. We're sorry to put you out like this."

Ed replied: "Listen, that's what I'm here for. How did things go for you after you went home? Were you able to get some rest?"

"Not really. Last night seemed like one long nightmare. I kept drifting off and then I'd jump and wake up and for a moment think that I'd been having a terrible dream. Then it would hit me . . ."

Mark choked up at that point and looked tearfully over to his wife.

"Jan, how are you doing right now?" Pastor Reid said quietly to Jan, who still had not looked at him. When she did look up her whole face seemed etched in pain, as if someone were reaching inside her and twisting her inner parts.

Commentary: Often, a counselor will follow the cues offered by a couple. This is especially true in the first stage of counseling. In this case, Mark directed attention toward his wife and the pastor followed. However, the pastor should be sensitive to patterns, such as Mark switching attention to his wife if he starts to get emotional. It is important to be able to tolerate the expression of emotions by others. The pastor, often encountering people in their moments of deepest pain and need, is challenged to remain connected with them, responding to them, while exposed to their intense feeling. A pastor's own emotions will also be aroused by these events and it is important for a pastor to process his or her own reactions in a safe place.

"I just, I just can't believe it. Not Karen. Of all people not Karen."

Pastor Reid immediately knew what she meant. He thought of all the faceless casualties he read about in the paper every day, the criminals who got shot by other criminals; but Karen was an energetic, talented, and likable highschooler; the kind of person you would never associate with death, about whom people would repeat the cliché, "she had her whole life ahead of her." The pastor also knew that it was hitting him hard because his own daughter was the same age and very much like Karen. They were friends in the church youth group. He found his mind imposing the face of his own daughter on Karen when thinking about the accident, and he even caught himself almost substituting his daughter's name as he talked to the Jacobsons. He forced himself to concentrate on the two people sitting in front of him.

Commentary: The pastor's emotions were activated by their story. In listening and being with them, the pastor felt vulnerable, felt the pain of his potential loss (the initial evidence of secondary trauma). He is challenged to be available to the couple, responding to them while managing his own experience.

"There are so many things we have to be doing to make arrangements, I just don't know where to start," said Mark.

"Listen, we'll have time to talk about that, but I really want to see what we can do to take care of you right now. You've just been plunged into a crisis. Can you tell me what has been happening to you since last night? Do you want to tell me what you know about what happened?"

Commentary: Mark, in an apparent attempt to protect himself from feeling the pain, begins to focus on the work to be done outside the counseling session. The pastor acknowledges Mark's protective response and chooses to redirect him back to the reality of their situation. In doing so, the pastor is gently nudging them to address the demands of reality by facilitating the sharing of their own experience. Encouraging them to tell their story begins the journey toward accepting reality. Often, the same story must be told many times.

Pastor Reid was a little surprised that it was Jan who spoke up. He could tell that a part of her really wanted to talk about the tragedy despite her intense pain.

"They were coming back from their grandparents, late. Too late. I had told her on the phone that they should think about staying at Grandma and Grandpa's . . ." Jan started sobbing. It took her a couple of minutes to collect herself during which her husband rubbed her back. The pastor decided not to say anything. "If I, if there was any way I could have demanded that they not drive back so late . . . we wouldn't be here now. Everything would be the way it should be." Jan started weeping again.

Commentary: It is common for a mourner to quickly attribute responsibility for the loss, to try to find some sense for cause or blame. Such attributions of responsibility are rarely realistic. Often, mourners will blame themselves, for then they have an illusion of control or influence in their situation. Ultimately, these attempts will prove futile, for things will not "be the way it should be"—the loss has permanently occurred.

After a minute or two Mark continued. "She fell asleep, Jack wasn't watching the road at the time, and they just plowed into a tree. They don't know, but they think she must have died right away."

Pastor Reid helped them continue to tell "the story" by asking about how they were contacted, what they found when they got to Jack in the hospital, how he was doing. "Jack's okay, thank God," was Mark's response, but Jan's response seemed enveloped in fear. Evidently at the hospital Jan alternated between being in shock and hugging Jack, calling him "her baby" with a frightful tone in her voice. Mark had told Jack that they were going to have to be strong for Mom.

During their talk Mark referred frequently to his concern for Jan. In his own way he looked more afraid than sad. The pastor noticed that Mark was hesitant to say much at all about Karen or the accident. In fact, his focus was very much on what was going to happen from now on. "Jack will be okay," he said more than once, but frequently, "I don't know what we're going to do for Jan." She basically seemed oblivious to Mark.

Commentary: The gender differences in responding to loss were illustrated in Jan's initial focus involving holding on to what she had and expressing her immediate feelings. The males in her family, on the other hand, appeared to shore each other up, to define what they needed to do, to focus outside themselves, and to ignore each other's reactions. It is likely that neither gender will initially understand the reactions of the other. The pastor may acknowledge the normalcy of each type of initial response.

Toward the end of their talk Pastor Reid was beginning to think that Mark was downright evasive when talking about Karen and the accident. He seemed very anxious to fix everything. The pastor decided to reserve judgment on it all and wait to see how Mark would be reacting during the days ahead. He also made a mental note of how little concern there seemed to be about Jack, especially from Mark. Was it due to the shock of the loss of Karen? That would be understandable. Was there almost too much attention being focused on Jan? After all, she was the one most capable of telling the story. And how is Mark really doing? Is he stepping in as protector? Or is he sidestepping his own loss? Pastor Reid decided that this was not the time to pursue any of those issues. They were still reeling from the shock of trauma, their grieving had hardly begun. Perhaps two or three weeks after the funeral would be about the right time to give them an opportunity to talk.

Jan spoke up and said that there was something very important to her that she needed to ask. She looked the pastor right in the eye and spoke calmly and deliberately.

"I have to know, pastor. About heaven. I don't really understand . . . is Karen in some kind of sleep now, or is she in the presence of God?"

Pastor Reid was taken off-guard by the question. He thought it was a good sign that despite Jan's tremendous loss she was thinking of Karen's welfare. He answered her question slowly and deliberately, explaining that the Scriptures do speak of the believer going immediately into the presence of God, but that there is no detailed explanation of what the experience is like—after all, how could we understand, from our earthly point of view. In any case, the Bible is perfectly clear that those who have "fallen asleep in Christ" are in a better state. Jan seemed comforted by the discussion, although she said very little.

Commentary: The pastor was sensitive to Jan's needs. Jan was searching for reassurance, not a theological or abstract discussion. The pastor is attempting to engage Jan in the reassurance, to increase her ownership of the experience.

"Yes, I do. I do know that Karen has always believed, and that she was looking for the right thing in her life. I just had to ask because now . . ." She couldn't finish her sentence, but Ed could tell she was thinking about the abrupt and absolute line drawn between life and death. "Can all this be real?" Jan whispered.

Pastor Reid asked Jan and Mark if there was anything specific they would like him to pray about before they left. "Yes," Jan spoke up, looking Pastor Reid straight in the eye, "pray that I wake up and this is all a dream." Her tone was at once sorrowful, angry, and insistent. "I wish I could pray that, Jan," Ed responded.

"I guess we should pray for the funeral," Mark said.

Commentary: Jan's reaction of anger and unrealistic demands and hopes are very common. The pastor was very helpful in allowing her expression without comment. Mark's reaction also is common during the initial adjustments to the loss. Again, he appears to be defending himself by focusing on the work to be done. This may be necessary for him at this time to make his initial adjustments to the loss.

"One of the things I've learned about prayer is that it sometimes just amounts to letting God hear our crying and our groaning," Ed said. "I want you to try to remember in the next few days that whenever you feel like it you can simply say 'heavenly Father,' and then whatever is on your heart, or just cry. God hears you and he will be near you even when you don't feel like he is."

Ed waited to see if the hard "why" question would come up at this point, but it didn't. It seemed as though they were able to accept at face value what he was telling them, and that it's what they wanted to hear.

Pastor Reid arranged for a time the next day for him to come to their home to plan the funeral and answer a few questions they had about the funeral home. He made a deliberate point to tell them that he wanted to stay in touch with them after the funeral, that he would contact them a couple of weeks after it to arrange a time to meet. He told them that the funeral would be hard, but it would be a very important time for them, and that he would do his best to help them and to show respect for the goodness of Karen's life. He also told them that some people in the church were volunteering to provide meals and asked them if it was okay with them for someone to organize that for them. Jan and Mark seemed pleased at the offer and agreed.

By the time they left Jan seemed calmer although washed out. Mark seemed about the same as when they came in, and left the office walking more slowly than when they came in.

Commentary: This session was likely as emotionally draining for the pastor as it was for Mark and Jan. He was successful in directing attention to the initial definition of the counseling problem and established a counseling relationship. The session may impact him in a number of ways. He may feel helpless, unsure of the value of what he offered, or questioning if he has anything to offer. His own fears and insecurities may become more evident. Thoughts such as buying a safer car or not letting his daughter drive at night may cross his mind. He also may experience a renewed awareness of how much he loves his own children. Ed would benefit from talking with a trusted colleague as he begins his own adjustment process.

8

Sessions 2, 3, and 4—
The Engagement Stage

Pastor Reid expected that the funeral would be difficult, and he was right. A couple of hundred people came during the visitation turning it into a community event. Whereas at most visitations there is a highly charged emotional moment when the immediate family gathers, at this one there was an almost continual spiking of the emotion in the room as more relatives and friends filed past the casket, which was closed but had a collection of photographs of Karen on it. Those closest to Karen invariably burst into tears and sobbing. It was obvious that many of the teenagers from her school had never been to a visitation before. Many of them looked frightened and stunned, walking past the casket with a breathless anxiety.

The funeral itself was longer than usual, although the pastor tried to convince the family and friends that a funeral that was too long with music and testimonials may be counterproductive. There was audible weeping throughout the funeral and lots of nose blowing, especially at the end of the songs. The three high school friends who gave eulogies rambled a bit, mostly pouring out their own emotion and putting Karen in a highly idealized position. As Pastor Reid stepped forward to give the message his body felt heavy, but felt

179

more energized as he began to speak and sensed the focused, almost piercing, attention coming from the rather large congregation. It struck him that he had never had, and maybe wouldn't have again, such attentiveness from teenagers, including his own daughter. At the end of it all he had that familiar but odd contradiction of feelings after a funeral: the sorrow of tragic loss, but the gladness of witnessing a dignified and loving ritual of mourning that validated the life of the deceased, and gave real hope for eternal life.

Commentary: A closed casket can interfere with accepting the reality of the loss, the finality of the death. When possible, viewing the lifeless body assists the breaking of the denial and strengthens the reality and acceptance of the loss.

Session 2

Two weeks after Karen's funeral Pastor Reid called the Jacobsons and set up a time the following week for them to talk. It struck Ed how vacant Jan's voice sounded on the phone. A home that usually had a lot of noise in the background was now quiet. She neither resisted the idea of talking nor sounded glad for the opportunity. Ed decided that he probably shouldn't expect anything more. When he asked about Mark, Jan said that she was sure he could come although he was very busy catching up with a lot of work.

When they sat down in the two chairs in front of Ed he immediately had a flashback to three weeks earlier when they sat there the morning after the accident. Mark looked sad and frightened then, now his face showed more tenseness, even anxiety. His jaw was clenched and there was a slight twitching of his temple. He seemed fidgety and looked at his watch several times during the conversation.

Three weeks before Jan had looked stunned and full of anguish, now her face looked frozen in sorrow. It seemed like there were deep lines where there hadn't been any before. And there was a slight frown in her expression, eyebrows angled down slightly. Ed thought to himself that if he didn't know who this woman was he would guess her to be either a very disappointed or a very angry woman.

Commentary: Ed has done a good job reading body language, or the nonverbal information that is shared. Much of the information about a person's experience is gained by observing his or her nonverbal, physical cues. In responding to this, Ed may increase his connection with the couple. A second source of information about another person's experience and the dynamic of a situation is the counselor's internal, subjective reactions. These are also monitored by Ed. The counselor needs to check his or her own subjective experiences against other data. Often, the "gut reactions" are very helpful in connecting with another person.

"Well, I'm glad we were able to work out a time to get together," Ed said. "I've been thinking a lot about you since the funeral."

"I suppose you noticed that we weren't in church the past couple of Sundays," Mark said. "The first week we were actually all ready to go, and then, well . . ."

"I couldn't go," Jan spoke up. "I wanted to, and I suppose I could have forced myself, but I thought that I would probably sit there in the pew and blubber like an idiot."

Commentary: Jan is expressing the emotion of shame and the fear of shame. As is common, she anticipates she will not be understood and is painfully aware no one else has the same reactions to this event she does—no one else was Karen's mother. Her pain from her loss magnifies her perception of being disconnected. Grieving people are so overwhelmed with the intensity of their own experience that they often sense they do not know how to respond to others. She has used self-critical remarks to keep self in control, to attempt to hide herself and minimize her vulnerability. Ed may have chosen to normalize the situation by stating such feelings are common and will be temporary. Many who are grieving avoid familiar places or situations that may expose vulnerability. Knowing this is common may decrease the feelings of shame.

"Would you find that embarrassing?"

"I suppose, but the harder thing is knowing that people wouldn't understand."

"Wouldn't understand what?"

"How it feels. What it's like. Nobody understands." Ed could sense the disappointment in Jan's voice. He made a mental note that it would be important to come back to the issue of their social relationships, but at the moment he wanted to focus on Mark and Jan.

"Can you tell me what you've been experiencing since the funeral?" Ed asked.

"By the way, Pastor," Mark chimed in, "we wanted to tell you how much we appreciated how you handled the funeral and every-thing. A lot of people commented to us about it. It was a very beau-tiful service." Jan nodded as Mark spoke.

"I felt privileged to be able to do it, although I regretted, as many people did, having to say goodbye to Karen. As awful as this whole thing is, I know you know that Karen is in the loving care of God and that you can look forward to seeing her again."

Commentary: Mark has again used a defense mechanism to pro-tect himself. He has changed the subject, moving away from emo-tionally charged issues. The pastor can note this and then choose whether to bring this to the person's attention or to follow his or her lead.

"Yes," Mark said, looking lost in his thoughts.

"How have you been doing, Mark?" Ed asked.

Jan gave a look of curiosity in Mark's direction as if wondering what he was going to say.

"I think I'm doing pretty well, all things considered. Work piled up, obviously; so I've been trying to dig my way out of that. I've been trying to be around the house in the evenings, canceled a busi-ness trip, so I could be with Jan. There has also been a lot to do with getting Jack out of the hospital and getting his room set since he'll be bed-ridden at home for at least a couple more weeks."

As Mark spoke Ed found himself wondering what may be behind Mark's words. On the one hand, there wasn't anything inappropri-ate about what Mark was saying, but still, he said hardly anything about Karen or the accident. He seemed hesitant to say anything about his own sorrow or grieving, yet Ed didn't want to jump to any conclusions, and he certainly didn't want to be in the position of being a crowbar.

Commentary: At this point, Ed has decided to confront Mark's defensive pattern. He is purposefully redirecting Mark's attention to the reality of the loss and Mark's personal experience. Note that Ed did not provide any interpretation or overt confrontation. Rather, a subtle comment was less threatening and hence more effective.

"Do you find yourself thinking about Karen much?" Ed asked.

"Oh, sure. Every now and then I can almost hear her voice in the next room, and then the incredible thought hits me, that she's gone. I find myself daydreaming, too. I'm sure that will change over time, don't you think?"

"Well, if grief is anything, it is a process. It's a kind of passage-way through which you go to get from one configuration in your life to another. When you lose someone very important, it's a huge change, and probably a complex and long-term process."

Commentary: Part of the pastoral counselor's role is to provide education, or information that will help them understand their experience, to have a definition of what is happening to them, the beginning of their changed schemata, their new worldview. Such education is most often best presented not in classroom format but in bite-size nibblets. The information is given in response to the expressed needs of the moment.

Ed noticed that Mark was trying to understand, but Jan seemed indifferent to these words.

"How long a process?" Mark asked, glancing at Jan.

"That's what almost everyone wants to know, Mark. Grieving is not something we want to do, for understandable reasons. We don't want to feel pain. But the pain started for you when Karen was killed. If you love someone you lose there is no way it isn't going to feel like agony. You also have a lot of adjusting to do. It takes time to do that."

There was an awkward silence as Mark seemed to shut down, and Jan was thinking about something different. Ed didn't want the conversation to go too far without Jan's involvement so he turned to her.

Commentary: Ed experienced an inner tension and appeared to be concerned that Mark and Jan may withdraw into their own pain, away from others. He observed that each was grieving individually. He chose to draw Jan in, knowing that in her pain she needed to remain connected.

"Jan, how have you been doing in these difficult days?"

Jan hesitated in responding, looking more reluctant than incapable. "Horribly. It's like my whole life has been taken away . . . what happened to her . . . it's just torn me up. What am I left with? My life is over as far as I'm concerned."

Ed resisted the temptation to catalog her blessings. He could tell that the problem was not a lack of perspective on her part, but the sheer trauma of having her only daughter torn out of her life.

"What do you find yourself thinking about in these days?" Ed asked.

Commentary: Ed has been facilitating the telling of her story and helping her express herself without interpretation or challenge from him. This is what Jan needs at this time, to connect with another through telling her story. This will eventually lead to connecting with herself, others, and God as she adjusts to her loss.

"I feel like my head has been scrambled. I can't concentrate on anything. I don't want to think about anything. I think about Karen a lot."

"About the accident, or about Karen herself?"

"No, not so much the accident. I find myself recalling conversations we had—I can almost remember them word for word; and what we used to do together . . . shopping, playing piano, cooking . . ." At this Jan began to cry hard and deep. "We really were friends, you know. A lot of mothers and daughters can't say that, but we really were friends. I miss her so much." Jan started weeping again, holding her abdomen as if the tears were coming from there. Mark put his hand on her back, face down, looking lost. Jan's weeping continued for a minute or two and then very gradually tapered off. She took several deep long breaths and grew very calm, but still subdued.

Commentary: As is common, Jan's story is over-idealized. Initially following a loss, people often try to connect with the good of what was but is now lost. This early task in the readjustment process facilitates moving away from avoiding the reality of the loss. Rando's theory defined this as the third task, the recollecting and reexperiencing of the deceased and the relationship.

"It is wonderful, Jan, that you and Karen had that kind of relationship. It's wonderful, too, that we all had the chance to know such a great kid. You have every reason to be proud of her."

"Maybe this would all be easier if Karen had not been a great kid," Jan said.

"Then you probably would have had a different kind of grieving. Jan, one of my favorite quotes is one from C. S. Lewis who said that the only place you can go to escape the pain of loss is hell, because there is no love there. In other words, when you have the blessing of a loving relationship, you have more to lose. Although, as you know, because we have hope, our loss as believers is limited and temporary."

"If I didn't know that, I'm not sure what I would do. I think I'd go crazy."

"Jan—and you too, Mark—one thing to realize right now is that in your hearts there is simply one thing that you want—for Karen to be back. You know that can't happen, and realizing that again and again is what is going to cause you to hurt. You are adjusting to a new reality. You've said that you feel very alone at times, and that's understandable. But rest assured that there are lots of people around you who love you. I've heard from numerous people how they want to help you. I want you to know that I am available to you at any time, to talk or pray, or just be with you. And God is with you, even when you have a hard time sensing it. If there is one thing he has told us again and again, it is that he will not abandon us."

Commentary: Ed is offering a reality contact, something that Jan and Mark can connect with. They are only minimally able to respond to these truths. However, hearing them at this time is beneficial for later adjustments. This is only one of many reminders of truth and hope he will provide them.

"Thank you, Ed," said Mark. "Sometimes I just don't want to be around other people, though. I'm not sure how helpful it is."

"What do you mean?" Ed asked.

Mark struggled to explain. "I don't know, they kind of fumble around, they try to make you feel better, which they can't. I think I'd do better just trying to get back to the way things were."

"I know what you mean about people being clumsy and awkward, but what do you mean 'by the way things were'?"

"I don't know, we have always been such a stable family. Hardly a bump in the road. I just want to be that way again."

"In other words, he wants his wife to be happy," Jan said a little sarcastically.

Mark stared straight at Ed.

"You want to have a happy family again?" Ed asked.

"Of course I do."

"How are you going to get there?"

"I don't know. I don't know. All I keep seeing is that car. I wish I'd never gone to the junkyard—that was a big mistake."

"Why?"

"The whole thing was mangled like it had gotten caught in some huge machine: torn metal, broken glass absolutely everywhere, one of her shoes still on the floor, and blood, lots of blood . . ." At this Mark began to cry. "I'm just glad Jan didn't have to see that." His crying came out in jerks. Ed thought to himself that whereas Jan's crying flowed out, sometimes in a trickle, sometimes in a rush, Mark's was coming out of an inner wrestling, but with what?

Commentary: Mark needs to tell his story as well. His experience is different than his wife's, as each person has a unique experience. Ed has directly challenged Mark to identify how he will reach his goals (a happy family). In doing so, he was responsive to what would reach Mark. This would have likely been inappropriate with Jan. Ed could have used this as an opportunity to ask Mark if he has any male support. Often, men do not have a friend with whom they can share such things. However, when challenged to think of one man who he could share with, many men are able to identify someone they could connect with. In such situations men should be encouraged to share with another man their experience.

Mark indicated that they needed to leave soon for an appointment with Jack's doctor, so Ed closed the session by asking them to relax and just listen carefully to some words of Scripture. He read slowly and quietly. Jan seemed to hang on the words and Mark, his face twitching a little, looked at the Bible as Ed read from it.

Ed told Jan and Mark that a friend of Karen and Jack had offered to cut the grass, and that a lady had offered to give Jan a car ride whenever she needed it. They thanked Ed and said the grasscutting would help, and that Jan would bear the ride offer in mind.

Ed prayed for Jan, Mark, and Jack before they left. He told them he admired their courage, and that he thought they were doing well under very trying circumstances. He reminded them that they could call him whenever they wanted to, and that he would like to call them a few weeks down the road and perhaps get together to talk again.

Session 3

The next time they met in Ed's office was three months after the funeral. Ed had called them a couple of times in between Sessions 2 and 3 to see how they were doing and to offer assistance. He also saw them in church, although they attended rather sporadically and seemed to avoid contact with other people. Ed got concerned when he heard from one of Mark's friends that Mark was talking about quitting his job and transferring to another location. Ed called and offered to talk again and Mark seemed eager to accept the offer.

This time Jan sat there looking washed out and weak. She looked like she had aged ten years in the last three months. She stared rather blankly, bumping herself on the desk as she took her seat, but seeming oblivious to it.

Ed was aware of how discouraged he himself felt. He was wrestling with a fear that if he asked many substantive questions he would find out Jan was getting worse, not better in her grief. *Have I missed something? Should another approach have been taken with this family? Do they sense any compassion from me or from this church?* Yet as soon as the question came into his mind about the length of mourning, he immediately remembered that, given this kind of loss, three months can be just the beginning of the process.

"Well, I'm glad to have a little more private time to talk to the two of you," Ed said. "You are on my mind virtually every day. How have things been going for you?"

Commentary: Pastor Reid has been aware of how Mark and Jan's circumstances have impacted him. Considering their situation, he has been confronted with his own vulnerability and has wondered if he is adequate, if he can offer something meaningful. He cannot take away their pain or undo their loss. He purposefully reaches out to them, resisting any temptation to withdraw, hide, or protect himself by becoming distant. At such a time, a pastoral counselor may struggle with either underinvolvement or overinvolvement. In modulating their own subjective experiences, pastoral counselors will be challenged to mature in their own faith.

Mark and Jan exchanged looks that appeared to say, "should you tell him or should I?" Mark cleared his throat and began. "On the whole, I'd say that things are going pretty well. Jan, we have discovered, has slipped into a depression—a clinical depression our family doctor called it—and has just in the past two weeks started taking some medication." Ed could sense that it was awkward for Mark to be talking about it.

"I'm so sorry to hear that, Jan," Ed said. "I am glad that you've been able to find medical treatment as necessary, though."

"Yeah, I'm still not sure I understand all that," Mark replied. "Somehow I never imagined one of us needing medical treatment to deal with our loss."

"Did you ever imagine you'd lose your only daughter?" Ed asked.

"No, of course not." Mark said.

Commentary: Ed recognizes that Jan's depression is a function of her being depleted by the loss. He does not look for blame, to determine what she has done (or not done) that led her to becoming depressed. He conceptualizes this as a consequence of the loss and demands for adjustment that have depleted, exhausted her biological coping resources rather than pathologizing her situation. Jan indicates that she is just now beginning to respond to the antidepressant medications. It is common for these medications to take two weeks to have any effect. As she has expressed, she may have more energy, feel less dysphoric, and notice her thoughts are more clear and focused, but she still has the same challenges and needs as before. These medications do not make one feel high or good but rather may be understood to replenish needed, normal brain chemicals so that the person has the biological resources to function. These medications were not intended to treat her grief process but rather to address her depression. Grief does not require psychological or medical treatment; her depression, if left untreated, could interfere for months or longer with her grief work. It is not uncommon for a family physician to prescribe antidepressant or antianxiety medications. These treatments are not to be used instead of counseling but as an adjunct, a resource that can increase one's effectiveness in working in and benefiting from counseling.

"It is so hard," Jan said quietly. "And I don't think it's getting any easier."

"Can you tell me what you mean?"

Jan shrugged, paused a moment, then her face pinched up in a bitter cry. "I still see her, hear her. I still find myself thinking I'll just wake up from a bad dream. I hurt so badly."

Ed let Jan cry and as he pushed the box of tissues closer to her he had a flashback of doing the same exact thing the two previous times here in the office. Now the question really hit him: How long, O Lord? How long must this mother suffer? It had been a long time since Ed felt so powerless. Yet he kept reminding himself that he was sitting across from victims of true trauma. Sure he wanted to take their pain away; but, he thought, how unnatural it would be for them not to be in a lot of pain a mere three months after the death of a daughter.

"I'm not at all surprised to hear you say that, Jan. As a matter of fact, a great many people going through the same circumstances would feel exactly the same way. You've faced one of the greatest losses a person can experience, the death of a son or daughter."

"But I thought I had more faith, more hope."

Commentary: Jan is displaying loss of hope, decreased self-esteem, negative thinking, and blaming herself in an attempt to make sense of her situation. Her schemata have been inadequate to account for her situation and she is struggling to regain a sense of understanding, meaning, and personal control. The pastoral counselor can help here by reframing her experience, identifying the reality of her painful feelings and questions while identifying unrealistic or inaccurate conclusions or self-critical judgments she derives.

"I'm sure you do have very substantial faith and hope. As a matter of fact, having known the two of you over the years, I know you do. One of the things you have to bear in mind is that, if you have gotten depressed to the point that it is affecting your very physiology, then that is going to have a dampening effect on the feelings of faith. It's like walking around with dark sunglasses on."

"I shouldn't be so depressed. I'm no good for anybody, for anything."

"It's not your fault that you are depressed, Jan. It's just the way it is for you right now. And it's not the way you'll always feel. Some of the greatest biblical figures like Elijah, Job, and Jeremiah got depressed when they were brought face to face with real trauma. The same is true for some of the great spiritual leaders like Martin Luther and Charles Spurgeon; or national leaders like Abraham Lincoln. I suspect that in some ways you are exercising a great deal of faith these days just by going on."

Ed turned to Mark. "Do you think you understand more about the real trauma that came into your lives three months ago?"

Commentary: Pastor Reid is attempting to engage Mark where he is, at the level of his intellect. In doing so, he opens a door for Mark to begin to express himself and allow himself to be connected.

"The last three months have seemed like three years," Mark said. "I just don't know where it's all going."

"Mark, one of your friends out of concern for you mentioned that you've been contemplating some changes."

Mark hesitated before responding. "Yes, I have been talking to Jan about whether we'd be better off getting a new start somewhere else. This town and the house we live in are now so full of sadness."

"Is this something you both want to do?"

"No, not Jan. But then, I think I might need to take some responsibility here since Jan is in no shape . . . well, to make any major decisions."

"I don't like the idea," Jan said, "and it's not because I'm incapable. Sure I know that Karen's empty room keeps hitting us in the face, but I also think I'd carry my sadness with me if I moved out of town."

"You're probably right," Ed said.

"I really don't want to add loss on top of loss. I know Mark means well, but if I lost my house, my neighbors, my church . . . it would all be too much."

"Well, there's nothing set in concrete," Mark said. Ed reiterated to Mark that any significant life changes add stress, and that, under the circumstances, there would have to be some pretty compelling reasons why they had to make such changes—and running away from grief is not one of them.

Commentary: Ed has become more directive in this explanation of Ed's assessment of Mark's plans. This type of intervention is the result of building the foundation of both their relationship as well as Ed's listening to Mark. Mark may now be ready for this feedback as he likely senses connection with Ed. A directive intervention prior to Mark's expression of his experience would likely have inhibited expression by Mark and blocked further responsiveness to Ed's input. Mark's desire to flee following a great loss or trauma is common. This desire may be a means to escape or avoid reminders of the loss. Mourners and traumatized people may benefit from counsel that encourages them to not make significant changes immediately following the loss or trauma. Such changes are often later regretted.

Jan mentioned that she knew these were real concerns for Mark—after all, he still had a hard time eating at the dinner table with the rest of the family and avoided it whenever he could.

"What about that?" Ed asked.

"I just can't stand seeing Karen's empty place, that's all," Mark said, a little defensively.

"That too is not uncommon for people mourning after a death," Ed said, "but that also points out to me that you are still very much in the midst of the grief process."

Ed asked Mark, and then Jan, what thoughts they had after reading the small book he recommended to them last time. Jan said it made her cry a lot, Mark said it raised a lot of questions. Ed let Mark ask his questions and gave each as good a response as he could.

Commentary: Mark's questions are a window to where he is in his adjustment process. Ed could have asked Mark to share the answers, albeit partial answers, he had already considered. In doing so, Ed would facilitate further expression and assist Mark in owning his own experiences, his thoughts and feelings. Mark is likely to benefit more from exploring these issues from his own frame of reference rather than from the counselor's.

"But there is one question that comes back to me more than anything else," Mark said. "Who is responsible for this?"

"What do you mean?"

"Well, I've been over it a thousand times. We shouldn't have let her drive late at night; she should have known better; Jack should have known better; that stupid road should have been marked differently; I . . ." Here Mark began to choke up. "I should have gotten her a better car. You see, it's like torture. There are so many ways in which this whole thing could have been easily prevented, but now it's too late. We've been robbed." Mark's tone turned angry.

Commentary: Mark is demonstrating further grief work. He is fighting against reality, attempting to take control of an uncontrollable loss. His desperate attempts to undo allow him to acknowledge and express his anger. The object of his anger is diffuse; Mark is searching for some place to put his anger, something to be angry with. Ed is appropriate in not confronting Mark at this point, for to do so would have inhibited Mark and interfered with his grief work.

"I've turned it over and over in my mind, maybe it's all because we've slipped in our devotional lives," Jan said.

"Or maybe because I've been so busy . . . I should have spent more time with the kids . . ."

Ed asked follow-up questions as a way of getting Mark and Jan to flesh out what they meant and what they were feeling. Ed took a few minutes to explain why it is dangerous to assume that, because a tragedy happens, it must be a punishment from God for a specific sin.

It became more and more evident that Mark was still, figuratively speaking, sitting in that auto wreck. Ed felt puzzled as to how to respond to all this, and decided that he needed some more time and perhaps consultation with a fellow pastor before taking a particular direction.

Commentary: Pastor Reid had previously shared his reactions to the Jacobson's situation. Now he needed strategic help as he planned his next step. Collegial relationships provide for both needs.

The session closed with Ed once again reading Scripture and praying; and though he had the passing thought that it seemed far too simple a thing to do, once again he could see that Jan and Mark seemed to be drinking in the words.

"By the way," Jan said as they were heading out the door, "You should know that when we last left your office we had some hope. Thanks."

Commentary: Pastoral counselors often choose to close each session with Scripture and prayer. Doing so can provide a reality contact, a reference point. This is not a quick fix but rather a reframing of thoughts, feelings, and experiences. Reading a Scripture passage with no commentary may bring Scripture into their adaptation process, challenging them to find meaning in the words and message of the words.

Session 4

Five weeks after Session 3 Pastor Reid got a call from one of the lay leaders of the high school ministry about Jack Jacobson. It was now almost five months since the accident; Jack was fully recovered from his injuries and had been back in school for six weeks. Pastor Reid had visited Jack a couple of times in the hospital and had seen him casually at church since then, but this phone call was the first indication he had that Jack was having some kind of difficulty. The youth worker told the pastor that Jack was not behaving like himself. It wasn't just that he was sad or subdued in the aftermath of his sister's death and his own brush with death, but he was moody, irritable, and uncooperative. One of his friends at the church had confided in the youth worker that Jack had withdrawn from his normal friends and had been seen with a few kids at the school who were known for heavy drinking and drug use.

Pastor Reid called in the staff youth pastor, ascertained that he had seen changes in Jack but didn't really know what to do about it. The youth pastor suggested that perhaps he should try to take Jack out for lunch and see if he could get him to share what was going on. Pastor Reid said that he would get in contact with the parents.

Commentary: The pastoral roles offer many options that are not available for mental health counselors. The boundary issues are different for many pastors as they relate to counselees in multiple roles. The shepherding illustrated here allows Pastor Reid to have information from many sources, sources that would not have been available to a mental health counselor. These differences in boundaries can be beneficial at times but also can complicate a situation and possibly compromise trust. The pastor is advised to not put himself or herself in the middle of communication, to strive to have those who are concerned speak directly to the other when possible, and to clarify with the counselee information obtained elsewhere. These boundary considerations also prompt many pastors to not engage in long-term counseling since the counselor role, with the accompanying intensity of the relationship, very often inhibits or prohibits relating in other roles.

When Ed called the Jacobsons, Jan seemed relieved to have an opportunity to talk about Jack. She told Ed she didn't want to impose on his time, but if possible, she would like it if they could get together because she was really concerned.

Commentary: Jan displays some shame with regard to her needs. Often a pastoral counselor can provide some relief from this shame by giving permission for the counselee to have and express needs, and to provide reassurance.

When the Jacobson's came to Ed's office a few days later Ed noticed that Jan was looking better than the last time they had talked. She looked like she had more energy and wasn't so flat in her expression. Mark, on the other hand, still looked tense and stressed and there were dark circles under his eyes.

"Thanks so much for seeing us," Jan said as she sat down. "I imagine you're getting pretty tired of the trials of the Jacobson family."

"Not at all, Jan. I don't want you to feel hesitant about asking for help. As a matter of fact, if there is one thing most important for you to do when you are grieving, it is to be open to help and to seek it out. How have the two of you been since we last talked?"

"I think I'm doing better," Jan said. "I know I am, actually. When we last talked I was at a real bad place. There are some things that were going through my head that . . ." Jan shuddered a little, "Well, things I never thought I would contemplate." She paused for a moment before continuing. "I don't think we're out of the woods yet, but at least I'm functioning—able to take care of the house and go out, that kind of thing."

"What do you find going on inside yourself?" Ed asked.

"I still feel like there's a hole there, the place where Karen used to be. But now when I think about her at least some of the time I smile instead of cry."

Commentary: Jan is evidencing changes in her schemata, demonstrating that adaptation is occurring as she is able to have multiple emotional reactions to memories of her daughter. It is unrealistic to expect she will ever be free of the pain resulting from this loss.

However, she is already experiencing a diminished intensity and frequency of the pain and an increase in positive memories.

"And how about you, Mark?"

Mark hesitated, looking like he had to concentrate in order to formulate an answer. "About the same, I guess."

"You're looking kind of tired. Have you been feeling okay?"

"Actually I feel tired all the time. Not sleeping like I should, I suppose. I've had—we've had—a lot of things to get through. I guess you called because you were concerned about Jack, is that right?"

Ed reiterated to Mark what he had told Jan on the phone about what the youth worker had said and told him that he wanted to know if there was anything they thought the church could do for them.

"I don't know about Jack," Mark said. "I suppose you could say he's been affected by all this: after all, he could have died in that car too. I just don't know what any of us can expect of him. I think we just need to give him some time."

Jan jumped into the conversation. "It's not that I expect anything of him. I'm just concerned, *very* concerned about him."

"What kind of concerns do you have?" Ed asked.

Commentary: Mark is again defending, focusing attention away from himself in an attempt to protect himself from his own pain. Ed has chosen to redirect attention back to Mark, assisting Mark in acknowledging his own experience. At this point, Mark's defenses are not helpful as they continually function to avoid his own reactions and needs and are contributing to not adjusting.

"Well, is it normal for a teenager to wake up in the middle of the night shouting from a nightmare, dripping with sweat?" Jan glanced at Mark who was blushing.

Commentary: Jan has exposed a secret, with a tone of anger she has verbalized a problem that no one has previously acknowledged. We often want problems to go away, hoping they will resolve themselves. In many situations such a secret is more complex than the initial revelation. The pastoral counselor will need to listen and observe both Jan and Mark if he is to understand what is being shared.

"What does Jack tell you about his nightmares?" Ed asked.

"Nothing," Jan said. "He won't say a thing. I'm not sure whether to let on that we know what's happening, if that will embarrass him too much. When I have tried to talk to him he's snapped at me. That's not like Jack. He's irritable most of the time these days."

Commentary: It is likely Jack has not shared his concerns or experiences with others. Teenagers often do not know how to understand their symptoms and frequently fear being weird, odd, or unacceptable. Thus, they are likely to keep their reactions to themselves. When working with a teenager, it is often helpful to list some common reactions, breaking the ice and giving them an opportunity to acknowledge that this is happening to them. This initial connection can relieve some of the shame they may be feeling. It is also common for a survivor of a trauma in which another did not survive to experience what is termed *survivor's guilt.* Jack may unrealistically blame himself for living when his sister did not. He may have mixed emotional reactions, longing for attention, love, and acceptance while sensing he shouldn't ask for this while his parents are grieving. In addition, he is also grieving his sister's death. He very likely feels very alone. The survivor's pain may not be acknowledged because others believe he is not in pain (because he's so relieved he did survive): it may be self-imposed out of shame or unrealistic thinking, or the recognition of the pain may be inhibited by others (family members, friends) who are consumed by their own grief.

Ed told the Jacobsons that what they were seeing in Jack was probably the consequences of real trauma. He gave them a handout that describes the experience and aftereffects of trauma and explained it to them step by step. He suggested they reread the small book on grief and trauma that he had them read several months earlier because they may be able to understand it more.

Commentary: Pastor Reid has chosen to provide further education at this point as a way of helping them obtain meaning in this situation. After hearing a few more anecdotes about Jack's behavior around the house he told Jan and Mark that the youth pastor was going to try to sit down with Jack and see if he could build some safe bridges, and that he would try to ascertain whether Jack may need to see a professional counselor.

Mark asked why that would be necessary—after all, Jack was the lucky one; he came out of the crash a survivor. Ed told him that, left unchecked, the storm inside Jack as a result of his trauma could have damaging effects on his life, that there were many ways that a teenager could make bad choices.

Mark sunk back in his seat, seemed less tense, and nodded in agreement. It appeared to Ed that Mark suddenly looked less defensive; like he had acquiesced.

"You're right," Mark said. "I guess I've seen it too, but didn't want to admit it."

Commentary: More of the secret is revealed as Mark expresses his anger at Jack, angry that he had survived and still needed more. Such revelations are often shocking to the parent and would have seemed unthinkable prior to the loss. These reactions can be better understood when it is remembered that emotions are reactions to something else and not the definitive statement of objective reality. The pastoral counselor can now assist Mark in determining what he believes is wrong and what needs to change. In doing so, Mark will further adjust to reality. Many parents in similar situations so focus on the child that has died that they neglect the surviving child or children. For some, the pain of losing a child is so great that they fear parenting, fear the caring and emotional attachment involved. To protect themselves from this possible pain, this vulnerability, they may emotionally distance themselves and express anger when this is identified by the child, spouse, or counselor.

"In retrospect, it does seem to me that whenever we've talked about Jack, you've worked very hard—almost too hard—to put it all in the best, most optimistic kind of terms," Ed said.

"That's true," Mark said.

"Do you have any idea why?" Ed asked.

"Sure I do. You see, Jack and I are a lot alike. Almost everybody who knows our family comments on that. I suppose I assumed that he would cope with all this the same way I was trying to."

"Which was?"

"To go on. Look ahead. There's nothing I would like to do more than change the past, but I can't. The only way I know how to cope is to forget the past."

"Doesn't seem like that's working for Jack," Ed said. "I don't know what he thinks about during the daytime, but it sounds like he's still in that car crash when he sleeps."

"Yes. . . ," Mark said, and started crying.

Mark told Ed—and Jan for the first time—that he too had been having nightmares about Karen and the accident. In his dreams the scenes would all tumble together: he'd be at the hospital and Karen was in the bed; then he was in the back seat of the car behind Karen and Jack with the tree looming ahead; then he'd see her as a child with a cut face and blood streaming down. The dreams were terrifying and he often felt like he hadn't gotten enough sleep. He said he didn't dare tell anybody, most especially Jan and Jack, because he had to be strong for all of them.

"I haven't told anybody else this . . ." Mark said, "but going and seeing her body, so that no one else would have to . . . seeing her pretty face disfigured the way it was . . . that was hard, very hard. I keep seeing that face."

Commentary: Now the rest of the secret has been revealed. Mark's pain and flashbacks have led him to focus on others, deny, and withdraw. These defensive actions had initially allowed him some protection from the overwhelming situation but, over time, had interfered with his ability to adjust. With this secret revealed he can now continue his grief work. Mark had a trauma he did not share with his wife or son. He had identified the body and he needed to share and adjust to this experience. Now he has an opening to do this. Such flashbacks are common. An image of the loss may appear at a moment of quiet, while in a group of people, or in a dream. The image may play out a scene that has not been resolved or may serve as an attempt to connect with what was lost.

When Mark got through telling his story he looked washed out. Jan held his hand and tears were slowly streaking down her cheeks. She hugged him for a minute or two, and then they were both quiet.

Ed spoke up. "I have a feeling you've wanted to let someone know this for a long time, Mark."

Mark nodded, and cleared his throat. "The funny thing, though, is that it's really been just in the last six or seven weeks that I've been having these dreams. It took me by surprise, I guess, and I thought they would just go away."

Ed continued to ask Mark questions about his experience at the hospital, his dreams, and about what was going on for him in his waking hours. Mark now spoke very freely, his tone of voice was more relaxed; he seemed anxious to talk. Ed acknowledged Mark's love for Karen in a way that was similar to what was happening for Jan in session 2. He also addressed forthrightly the issue of guilt and shame that was obviously on Mark's mind whenever he swung back to the question of who was responsible for the accident. Mark seemed very eager to hear what Ed had to say about Mark's taking blame on his own shoulders. He also took in what Ed had to say about Mark's responses to Jack.

Commentary: Integrating flashback into the reality of experience can diminish the intensity of experience; the opposite, to suppress, would intensify the disconnection and the recurrent flashbacks.

As the session closed Ed read some Scriptures that related to the freedom of grace and forgiveness, a new theme in this counseling process. When he prayed for them Ed felt like the other two people in the room were really praying with him. They seemed less like passive victims and more like seeking children.

Ed told them that there was obvious movement in their grieving process, and that he admired them for how they were doing. He suggested that Mark try to reach out to Jack, perhaps confide in him that he too was experiencing flashbacks. He suggested that perhaps in a couple of months they could get together again, but that they should not hesitate to call on him or anyone in the church if needs arose in the meantime. He assured them that he would have the youth pastor do as much as he could for Jack and that he would phone them with his recommendation.

Commentary: The work of grief and the adjustments to trauma require one to tell and retell the story. As the stories are repeatedly told they change, the schemata are modified, the shame diminished, and the adjustments occur. Assimilation and accommodation occur through the telling and retelling of the stories, which leads to adaptation and acceptance.

9

Session 5—
The Disengagement Stage

At first Jack declined the opportunity to get together with the youth pastor but a couple of days later changed his mind. The youth pastor had an excellent rapport with the kids and, following Pastor Reid's advice, tried to give Jack a wide open door to share what was going on. Apparently Jack was relieved to have what seemed to be a safe person to talk to and revealed many of the details of his dreams, his recollections of the accident, and even some self-destructive thoughts he had been having. The youth pastor and Pastor Reid told Jack that it was very good that he was confiding in this way, but that they would like to draw a professional counselor into the process. With Mark and Jan's consent, and gratitude, Pastor Reid referred Jack for an initial session with a counselor.

Pastor Reid could tell over the phone that Mark and Jan both seemed more stable, and suggested that they get together one more time so that they could talk about what lay ahead for them. When they met it was two months after the last session, seven months after the funeral.

Session 5

The first thing that was on the Jacobsons' minds was what was going on with Jack. They wanted to know what would be happening, how long he would need to see a counselor, what they could and should do to help. Jack had seen a counselor for several weeks. Pastor Reid told them he thought it was a good sign that Jack was so quick to share once he started, but that there was no way to know how many times he ought to see the counselor. He used the opportunity to explain in more detail the dynamics of trauma, and to give the Jacobson's a realistic assessment of where Jack may be at. His near-death experience and the witnessing of the death of his sister a few feet away were inevitably going to be with him the rest of his life. The good news is that there are ways of coping, and that his faith would be able to help him with residual feelings of shame, anger, or fear.

Commentary: Pastor Reid's decision to refer Jack for specialized treatment was made in light of the indications of PTSD. The intrusive memories and accompanying physical arousal were inhibiting his current functioning. Such a decision to refer is made in light of both the counselor's assessment of his or her own skills and resources as well as the severity of symptoms. It is important to recall that the grief process does not need treatment, although complicated grieving may.

Mark told Pastor Reid that the counselor had suggested a joint session with Mark and Jack (Jan had been a part of the initial session). Pastor Reid told Mark he thought that sounded like an excellent idea, given the fact that there were many similarities between Jack's and Mark's reactions to the accident.

"Have you continued to have flashbacks to Karen and the accident?" Pastor Reid asked Mark.

"Occasionally," Mark replied. "But no where near as often as before. And the biggest difference is that I don't brood over it the whole next day. Jan is now well aware if I have a restless night and she has no problem talking with me about what I experienced."

Commentary: Mark now reports that his symptoms have diminished and he is able to talk about it. The shame he had felt is lessened following his expression. As is often the case, the intensity of the shame was lessened by exposing the shame. Now, the occurrence of flashbacks can be shared and the pain lessened by being connected with others, understanding what is happening, and letting go of the pain.

"I think we're a lot closer now," Jan said. "For one thing, I realize that before I thought I was the only one really suffering, but now I know that Mark has been mourning as much as I have."

"You feel less alone in your grief?" Pastor Reid asked.

"Exactly. The one thing I didn't need to have added to my sadness is loneliness."

"I guess I was assuming that my grief would pile up on top of Jan's, and she would just collapse under the weight of it all," Mark said.

Commentary: It is important for each spouse to recognize that the other suffered, that the loss impacted them both greatly. Both will mourn in their own fashion. Both need to express their experience, to identify how the loss has impacted them. Without doing so, connection between them is blocked and anger is likely to develop. Some spouses believe they need to keep secret their pain in order to protect their partner. This belief often results in further distance between the couple and a diminished sense of safety.

"That's a common assumption," Pastor Reid said. "But you see, the pain you feel in grief issues from the loss itself. The fact that you have been mourning yourself, Mark, doesn't really add to the pain—either way, Karen died in that accident. In fact, it appears that you've found that your grieving has been validating for Jan. She doesn't need to second-guess herself, wondering if her deep grieving meant she was doing something wrong." Jan was nodding as Pastor Reid spoke.

Pastor Reid mentioned that he had seen them around the church more often for special events, and the Jacobsons told him that they were starting to feel comfortable resuming some of their old activities. They just rejoined their midweek Bible study group and sensed that the group was very glad they were back. They did have some questions about how to respond to people who make insensitive and shallow comments, and to those who seemed frightened and avoiding. Though Pastor Reid could sense that Jan and Mark were still sensitive to those experiences, they at least seemed to understand the reasons people behave the way they do. He told them they were not really responsible for the actions of others, and that, for their own sakes, they should make sure they keep a wide open door to the two or three friends who had the most understanding.

Commentary: The issues of secondary victimization need to be discussed when the counselees hint at its presence. Validation of the pain caused by others' reactions can be helpful. In addition, Pastor Reid led them toward discerning between those who were safe and unsafe, those who understood and those who didn't, and to discern who was responsible for each. The reality of living in a sinful world is that not all relationships are safe. Pastor Reid was addressing their vulnerability toward victim thinking by helping them choose from several options in coping with these concerns.

As it turns out, it was one of Jan's old friends who was the first to reach out to her in a truly understanding way, and that she had confided in Jan that she had lost her younger sister in a car accident thirty years ago. She and Jan found such comfort in confiding in each other that they talked about starting a support group in the church for those who have experienced the sudden death of an immediate family member. Pastor Reid told Jan that he thought it was an excellent idea and that he would help them set it up when they were ready.

Commentary: Part of resolving a loss and finding meaning to one's life is to contribute in a meaningful way to others. Jan is demonstrating further adaptation by being able to reinvest in others. For many a support group is a means to this end.

"What are your thoughts about what lies ahead for the two of you in the future?" Ed asked.

"I think we're still going on the one-day-at-a-time plan you told us about at the very start," Mark said. "But I think we're more together as a family. I never would have thought it, but there was a while there when it felt like we were drifting apart."

Commentary: Statistically, Mark and Jan's marriage was at great risk following the death of their daughter. The pain, disconnection, and anger, if not resolved, could be directed toward each other and the relationship rather than in adjusting to the loss.

"I still feel like there's a big hole where Karen used to be," Jan said. "I'm not sure that's going to change. But before I used to feel like I was lost in that hole whereas now it seems more like a part of my life that is missing."

"There's a big difference," said Ed. "If you feel like you're being swallowed up by your loss, you're in a real crisis. If, on the other hand, your loss looks like a part of your life that has been removed, then you're dealing with reality. And the reality is that there are other parts of your life. Nothing will replace Karen in this life, but there are still many new things that God wants to bring into your life."

Commentary: Karen's death was not good. This trauma initially consumed her loved one's entire existence. As Mark and Jan are adjusting to their loss, they realize that their life is bigger than Karen's death, that their lives can have good in them. Their enjoyment of the good is not a commentary on their love for Karen. They can recognize that God is still active in their lives, and although they presently "see through a glass darkly," they can have a sense of peace that God continues to love them and is active in their lives.

Ed spent the remaining time reminding them of some of the words of eternal life spoken at the funeral—truths about the character of God and the reality of heaven. Both Jan and Mark said that they were more ready to take in the meaning of those words now.

Commentary: Pastor Reid, Jan, and Mark have begun the adjustment process away from their counseling relationship. Future contacts will be in the more general pastoral relationship in the various activities of the church community. They have focused on specific adjustment challenges and, at this time, have successfully made the transitions toward acceptance. Not all of their changes have occurred; they will continue to experience grief at times throughout their lives. Mark and Jan can now cope in the present with the reality of their loss. They are increasing in their ability to love and be loved.

References

Bolby, J. 1980. *Attachment and loss.* New York: Basic Books.

Cole, D. 1987. It might have been: mourning the unborn. *Psychology Today* 21(2): 64.

Cook, A. S. and Dworkin, D. S. 1992. *Helping the bereaved.* New York: Basic Books.

Donaldson, M. A. and Gardner, R. 1980. Diagnosis and treatment of traumatic stress among women after childhood incest. In *Trauma and its wake*, ed. C. R. Figley, pp. 356–77. New York: Brunner/Mazel.

DSM-IV (Diagnostic and Statistical Manual of Mental Disorders, 4th ed.). 1994. Washington, D.C.: American Psychiatric Association.

Eth, S. and Pynoos, R. S. 1985. Developmental perspective on psychic trauma in childhood. In *Trauma and its wake*, ed. C. R. Figley, pp. 36–52. New York: Brunner/Mazel.

Foa, E. B., Steketee, G., and Rothbaum, B. O. 1989. Behavioral/cognitive conceptualizations of post-traumatic stress disorder. *Behavior Therapy* 20: 155–76.

Goleman, D. 1992. Wounds that never heal. How trauma changes your brain. *Psychology Today* 25(1): 62–66.

Green, D. and Lawrenz, M. 1994. *Encountering shame and guilt.* Grand Rapids, Mich.: Baker Books.

Grove, D. J. and Panzer, B. I. 1991. *Resolving traumatic memories.* New York: Irvington Publishers, Inc.

Hamberger, L. K. and Lohr, J. M. 1984. *Stress and stress management.* New York: Springer Publishing Company.

Horowitz, M. J. 1979. Psychological response to serious life events. In V. Hamilton and D. M. Warburton (eds.), *Human Stress and Cognition.* New York: Wiley.

Jacobs, S. and Lieberman, P. 1987. Bereavement and depression. In O. Cameron (ed.), *Presentations of Depression.* New York: Wiley.

Keane, T. M. 1989. Post-traumatic stress disorder: Current status and future directions. *Behavior Therapy* 20:149–53.

Kubler-Ross, E. 1975. *On death and dying.* New York: MacMillan Publishing.

Kubler-Ross, E. 1975. *Death. The final stage of growth.* Englewood Cliffs, N.J.: Prentice-Hall.

Kulka, R. A., et al. 1990. *Trauma and the Vietnam War generation.* New York: Brunner/Mazel.

Knapp, R. J. 1987. When a child dies: how parents react to and cope with one of life's most devastating losses. *Psychology Today* 21(6).

Krystal, J. H., Southwick, S. M., Bremner, J. D., and Charney, D. S. 1992. Emerging neurobiology of post-traumatic stress disorder. *The Psychiatric Times* (August), 19–21.

Lewis, C. S. 1961. *A grief observed.* Toronto: Bantam Books.

Lew, M. 1988. *Victims no longer.* New York: Harper and Row.

Lindberg, F. H., and Distad, L. J. 1985. Post-traumatic stress disorders in women who experienced childhood incest. *Child Abuse and Neglect* 9:329–34.

Madakasirs, Sudhaker, and O'Brien. 1987. Acute post-traumatic stress disorder in victims of a natural disaster. *The Journal of Nervous and Mental Disease* 175: 286–92.

Matsakis, A. 1992. *I can't get over it. A handbook for trauma survivors.* Oakland, Calif.: New Harbinger Publications, Inc.

Murphy, S. A. 1986. Health and recovery status of victims one and three years following a natural disaster. In *Trauma and its wake,* vol. 2, ed. C. R. Figley, pp. 133–55. New York: Brunner/Mazel.

Pauck, Wilhelm, trans. and ed. 1961. *Martin Luther's Lectures on Romans.* Philadelphia: Westminster.

Piper, W. E., McCallum, M., and Azim, H. F. A. 1992. *Adaptation to loss through short-term group psychotherapy.* New York: The Guilford Press.

Rando, T. A. 1984. *Grief, dying, and death: Clinical interventions for caregivers.* Champaign, Ill.: Research Press.

Rando, T. A. 1993. *Treatment of complicated mourning.* Champaign, Ill.: Research Press.

Shalev, A. Y., Orr, S. P., and Pitman, R. K. 1992. Psychophysiologic response during script-driven imagers as an outcome measure in post-traumatic stress disorder. *Journal of Clinical Psychiatry* 53(9): 324–26.

Southwick, S. M., Krystal, J. H., Morgan, A., Johnson, D., Nagy, L. M., Nicolaou, A., Heninger, G. R., and Charney, D. S. 1993. Abnormal noradrenergic function in post-traumatic stress disorder. *Archives of General Psychiatry* 50:266–74.

Staudacher, C. 1987. *Helping those who grieve.* Oakland, Calif: New Harbinger Publications, Inc.

Staudacher, C. 1991. *Men and grief.* Oakland, Calif: New Harbinger Publications, Inc.

Webb, N. B. 1993. The child and death. In *Helping bereaved children*, ed. N. B. Webb. New York: The Guilford Press.

Westberg, G. E. 1962. *Good grief.* Philadelphia: Fortress Press.

Wilson, J. P., Smith, W. K, and Johnson, S. K. 1985. A comparative analysis of PTSD among various survivor groups. In *Trauma and its wake*, ed. C. R. Figley, pp. 142–72. New York: Brunner/Mazel.

Wolin, S. 1991. Discovering resiliency: children at risk. *The Addiction Letter* 7(11): 1–4.

Wolin, S. and Wolin, S. 1992. How to survive (practically) anything. *Psychology Today* 25(1): 36–40.

Wolin, S. and Wolin, S. 1993. The challenge model: discovering resiliency in children at risk. *The Brown University Child and Adolescent Behavior Letter* (March), 9:1–4.

Wolin, S. and Wolin, S. J. 1993. *The resilient self.* New York: Villard.

Worden, J. W. 1990. *Grief counseling and grief therapy: A handbook for the mental health practitioner*, 2d ed. New York: Springer.

Yancey, P. 1988. *Disappointment with God.* Grand Rapids, Mich.: Zondervan Publishing House.

Yancey, P. 1990. *Where is God when it hurts?* Grand Rapids, Mich.: Zondervan Publishing House.